D1714904

PLAYS FROM THE CYNICAL LIFE

THE WASHINGTON STRINDBERG
Translations and Introductions by Walter Johnson

Plays
from the Cynical Life

PLAYING WITH FIRE, DEBIT AND CREDIT
MOTHER LOVE, THE FIRST WARNING
FACING DEATH, PARIAH, SIMOON

by AUGUST STRINDBERG
Translations and Introduction
by Walter Johnson

University of Washington Press
Seattle and London

Copyright © 1983 by the University of Washington Press
Printed in the United States of America

Library of Congress Cataloging in Publication Data

Strindberg, August, 1849–1912.
  Plays from the cynical life.

  (The Washington Strindberg)
  Contents: Playing with fire — Debit and credit — Mother love — [etc.]
  I. Title. II. Series: Strindberg, August, 1849–1912. Washington Strindberg.
PT9811.A3J6   1983   839.7'26   82-13581
ISBN 0-295-95980-0

Preface

THE PLAYS IN this volume are all one-act dramas based on human situations as conceived and interpreted by Strindberg at a time when he was convinced human beings are essentially selfish, self-centered creatures. Two of the plays—*Pariah* and *Simoon (Samum)*—were written in 1889; the others were written in 1892 and labeled by Strindberg himself as "one-acters out of cynical life" (*"En aktare. Ur det cyniska livet"*). All of them, however, share the same gloomy view of human nature, human behavior, and human society.

Two plays that belong to this group—*The Stronger* and *The Bond*—were included in the volume entitled *Pre-Inferno Plays* (Seattle and London: University of Washington Press, 1970; and New York: W. W. Norton, 1976, paperback).

The Bond is an excellent treatment of divorce; both as drama and theater, it belongs with the great plays *The Father*, *Lady Julie*, and *Creditors* as one of the outstanding Strindberg contributions to naturalistic and realistic drama. The ones in this volume, however, should not be disregarded by any student of drama seeking to understand Strindberg's contribution. They offer, moreover, excellent challenges both to undergraduate and to professional actors who are looking for short, stageworthy plays.

The translations are based on the text in the Landquist edition of Strindberg's complete works. They are, I trust, idiomatic translations that are faithful to the original without being slavishly literal.

Walter Johnson

Contents

Illustrations

PLAYS FROM THE CYNICAL LIFE

Introduction to
the One-Act Plays

IN OCTOBER 1909, when Strindberg wrote a brief preface to then unpublished *Författaren (The Author)*, the fourth volume of his autobiography *Tjänstekvinnans son* (1886), he listed among his most important (*viktigaste*) works the one-act plays of the early 1890s as "one-acters out of cynical life." The item included *The First Warning, Debit and Credit, Facing Death, Mother Love, Playing with Fire*, and *The Bond*. He might just as well have included three one-act plays from the late 1880s: *The Stronger, Pariah*, and *Simoon*. All nine are short, stageworthy one-act plays; all were designed for production in experimental theaters; and all are interpretations of human situations from a cynical point of view.

Strindberg's hope of having a theater in which his plays would be produced seemed to have a chance of realization in the late 1880s in Copenhagen but did not materialize until the Intimate Theater opened in Stockholm in 1907. He had written his great plays—*The Father* (1887), *Lady Julie* (1888), and *Creditors* (1888)—deliberately as what might very well be segments of actual life with increasing emphasis on universal themes, avoidance of distracting factors such as intermissions, and simplification of staging. The one-act plays listed above are essentially further extensions of his "attempts to transform drama into a form suitable for the time" (*Samlade skrifter*, vol. 19, p. 148). They deal, moreover, with universal and timeless themes. The very brevity of these plays precludes examination in appreciable depth as in the longer

3

plays of 1887 and 1888, but they have enough detail to provide audience and reader with material for creative participation and involvement. In each there is enough irritating matter to arouse reaction and to stimulate discussion.

The human situations presented are surely typical: people's willingness to claim credit for a fellow human being's success, a mother's manipulation of her daughter's life, a wife's indifference to her mate except when others obviously want him, denigration of a mate for one's own purposes, indifference to and rationalization of one's sins, playing with one's own and others' emotions, and the unhesitating destruction of a fellow human being at least partly in the name of religion.

All of these matters fit in nicely with Strindberg's far from sentimental view of human nature and human society in the late 1880s and early 1890s. Under the influence of naturalism and "free thinking" at the time, he took a gloomy and pessimistic view of human motives and human behavior. People are, he then thought, selfish animals with only camouflaging masks of civilization and generally unacknowledged devotion to self-interest and self-indulgence.

Since success is rarely if ever merely the result of one person's own endeavors, a quick look at what happens to one human being on the verge of genuine achievement and general recognition is precisely what Strindberg gives us in *Debit and Credit* (1892). The earliest possible confrontations of the man who apparently "has it made" by people who either believe they helped get him where he is or by people who are more than ready to benefit from his "success" on his exploration of and study in parts of what then was darkest Africa. Brother, sister-in-law, former colleague and peer, a discarded girl friend, a woman eager to gain much through marriage to the man who apparently has arrived, and a displaced rival are all sufficiently revealed to make it interesting for the audience and the reader to speculate about debts and gratitude, debtors and creditors, and means of coping with such human dilemmas.

Facing Death (1892) is even gloomier in its implications about the family, the human institution Strindberg valued above all others. In one brief act we witness a marital hell in which a dead wife's evil, lingering presence brings about the suicide of her husband, and we are given a highly pessimistic view of child–parent relationships. The situations are clear enough, and audience and reader can creatively supply the necessary nuances. Some of the details (the bait in the rat trap and the milk in the cat's saucer, for example) will call for suspension of disbelief, even if children's deliberate cruelty and a dead wife's continuing presence have driven the father to such behavior as arson and suicide.

The role of jealousy within marriage is the subject of *The First Warning* (1892), an amusing consideration of the motives and behavior of a wife and a husband with the attendant dilemmas of marital irritations. The solution of the problems through the device of jealousy is reconciliation "for at least eight days." The "aging" wife who loses her first tooth, the husband who resents other men's attention to his mate, a precocious teenager infatuated with an older man, and an aging baroness who has lost her man because of jealousy all represent people who are essentially and primarily interested in their own emotional satisfaction and security.

Mother Love (1892) recalls *The Father* (1887) and the later *The Pelican* (1907) in its presentation of a mother's selfish manipulation of a daughter's life, but goes beyond the two longer plays in making the mother not only morally corrupt but also judged as such by the community. The two young women are challenging roles for actresses: a lovely daughter who has not been corrupted in her previous years by her mother's selfishness, bitterness, and vulgarity, and an unbelievably precocious legitimate half-sister.

Much more entertaining is the longer one-act drama, *Playing with Fire* (1892), a look at two older people and four younger ones who have the means to worry about little else but making their days pass as pleasantly as possible. At least four of them play with the fire of sexual attraction without serious meaning or consequences for any of them. *Playing with Fire* has been popular on the Swedish stage, more so than any of the other one-acters in this volume.

Pariah (1889) is the finest illustration of Strindberg's practice of dramatizing prose fiction, usually his own but in this little play a story by his friend and colleague, Ola Hansson (1860–1925). Interested at the time in crime and punishment, Strindberg presents an unintentional murderer and a forger who says he is not to blame in a confrontation that can justifiably be labeled a battle of brains. It is a very good little play, as Strindberg said, in the Edgar Allan Poe manner.

The briefer one-act play, *Simoon* (*Samum*, 1889) is, as Strindberg said in a March 10, 1889 letter to Ola Hansson, another "brilliant Edgar-Poe play" in which he presents an Arabian girl's psychic murder of a weakened French soldier through suggestion, hypnosis, and ventriloquism.

All of these plays, as well as *The Stronger* (1889) and *The Bond* (1892), both of which are included in the earlier volume *Pre-Inferno Plays*, are stageworthy, as actors in Sweden and abroad have found on numerous occasions.

Playing with Fire

A Comedy in One Act

Characters

THE FATHER, *a person of independent means, age 60*

THE MOTHER, *age 58*

THEIR SON *(Knut), an artist, age 27*

KERSTIN, *their daughter-in-law, age 24*

THE FRIEND *(Axel), age 26*

THE COUSIN *(Adele), age 20*

Setting

A glass-enclosed veranda that has been converted to a living room. A door leading to the garden and to the sides. At a resort in our day {the 1890s}.

The son is sitting painting. His wife, the DAUGHTER-IN-LAW, *dressed for the morning, comes in.*

SON: Is he up yet?

DAUGHTER-IN-LAW: Axel!—How could I know?

SON: I thought you looked.

DAUGHTER-IN-LAW: Shame! If I didn't know you could never be jealous, I'd begin thinking you are!

SON: And if I didn't know you could never be unfaithful, I'd begin pulling my ears!

DAUGHTER-IN-LAW: Why? Just now?

SON: You heard what I said: *if* . . . as far as our friend Axel goes, you know I don't appreciate anyone else's company as much as his, and when luckily you share my feelings for the poor torn soul everything's fine!

DAUGHTER-IN-LAW: He's an unhappy human being, but all the same he seems pretty strange occasionally. Why, for example, did he leave us so hastily last summer without even saying good-bye and without taking his things?

SON: Yes, that was strange! I thought he had fallen in love with Cousin Adele.

DAUGHTER-IN-LAW: You did?

SON: Yes, but I don't think so any more! Mother persuaded me he had gone back to his wife and his child.

DAUGHTER-IN-LAW: What? Aren't they divorced?

SON: Not quite, but he's expecting the decree any day.

DAUGHTER-IN-LAW: So you thought he loved Adele? And

you haven't said so before! Well, if they could get
together, that would be pretty good, I think.

SON: Who knows? Adele's a dud . . .

DAUGHTER-IN-LAW: Adele? Then you know her very little!

SON: She has a charming figure, but if she has any feelings,
any passions . . . I'll leave unsaid.

DAUGHTER-IN-LAW: If she has?

SON: Well, does she?

DAUGHTER-IN-LAW: Yes, when she once opens up . . .

SON: No, really!

DAUGHTER-IN-LAW: That seems to interest you?

SON: In a way!

DAUGHTER-IN-LAW: In what way?

SON: You know she was my model as the swimmer . . .

DAUGHTER-IN-LAW: Yes, I certainly know that. Who hasn't
been your model? But you could be considerate enough
not to show your sketches to everyone . . . There, the old
woman's here! (*The* MOTHER, *badly dressed with a big
Japanese hat and carrying a food basket.*)

SON: You look awful today, Mother!

MOTHER: You are polite!

DAUGHTER-IN-LAW: Knut is certainly terrible. But what have
you bought?

MOTHER: Oh, I got such superb flounders . . .

SON (*digging in the basket*): Good lord! But what's this?
Ducklings?

DAUGHTER-IN-LAW: They could have been a little fatter . . .
feel here under the breast.

SON: I think the breasts are lovely!

DAUGHTER-IN-LAW: Shame on you!

MOTHER: Well, you got your friend back, last night!

SON: Our? He's Kerstin's friend! She's absolutely crazy about
him! I thought they'd kiss each other last night when he
came!

MOTHER: Don't joke like that, Knut, for the one who plays with fire . . .

SON: I understand, but I'm too old, you see! Besides, do you think I look as if I need to be jealous?

MOTHER: It isn't how you look . . . isn't that right, Kerstin?

DAUGHTER-IN-LAW: I don't understand what you mean!

MOTHER (*strikes her lightly on the cheek*): You! Watch it!

SON: Kerstin's so terribly innocent and you, you old bat, mustn't spoil her!

MOTHER: You two have such a nasty way of joking, one never can know when you're serious!

SON: I'm always serious.

DAUGHTER-IN-LAW: A person could think so for you never laugh when you make your dirty remarks!

MOTHER: You're quarrelsome this morning, I think . . . Didn't you sleep well last night?

SON: We didn't sleep at all!

MOTHER: Shame on you! No, really, now I'll be on my way, otherwise Father will scold me.

SON: Father, yes! Where is he?

MOTHER: I suppose he's out taking his morning walk with Adele!

SON: Aren't you jealous?

MOTHER: Huh!

SON: Well, but I am!

MOTHER: Of whom? If I may ask?

SON: Of the old man, of course.

MOTHER: Kerstin, what a fine family you got into!

DAUGHTER-IN-LAW: Yes, if I didn't know Knut so well and if I hadn't known beforehand that artists are a special breed, I'd really not know what's what now and then.

SON: Yes, I'm an artist, but Father and Mother are philistines . . .

MOTHER (*without anger*): You're certainly a philistine, you

have never earned your own keep and are getting on in
years. And your father certainly wasn't a philistine when he
built this house for a good-for-nothing like you!

SON: One isn't the only son for nothing! Good-bye now or
you'll get your scolding *here*, and I don't want to listen to
that! Hurry up! The old man's coming!

MOTHER: Then I'll go out this way. (*Goes.*)

SON: There's a damnable draft in this house—a real cross
draft!

DAUGHTER-IN-LAW: Yes, in-laws could certainly give us a
little more peace; and then there's our having to eat at their
table and not have a household of our own . . .

SON: Just as when they put out food for the sparrows on the
window ledge—so they may have the pleasure of seeing
how they eat! . . .

DAUGHTER-IN-LAW (*listens intently*): Sh-h! Try to cheer up
the old man so we won't have to listen to their morning
bickering!

SON: If I only could! And he's not always in a mood for my
nice jokes!   (*The* FATHER *dressed in a white vest and black
silk jacket with a rose in his buttonhole comes in. The* COUSIN
enters, walks about at first, then starts to dust.)

FATHER (*without raising his hat*): It's cold this morning!

SON: I can see that!

FATHER: How can you see that?

SON: I see your head is cold at least! (*The* FATHER *looks
contemptuous.*)

DAUGHTER-IN-LAW: How shameless you are, Knut!

FATHER: A fool makes sorrow for himself, and a fool's father
has no joy.

SON: Where do you get all your sayings?

DAUGHTER-IN-LAW (*to* ADELE): I've dusted today, dear!

FATHER: Through wise women the house was built, but a
madman destroys it with his ways!

SON: Did you hear that, Adele?

COUSIN: I?

SON: Yes! Listen. Where can I find this proverb: "A beautiful woman without discipline is like a sow with a golden ring in her nose"?

DAUGHTER-IN-LAW: Knut, really!

FATHER: You got company late last night?

SON: Did you think it was too late?

FATHER: I think nothing! But—a young man could certainly choose a more suitable time for his visits.

SON: So, you think so anyway!

FATHER: Had you invited him?

SON: What sort of third degree is this? Maybe you have thumb screws along.

FATHER: No, you've taken over those! The least little question I ask, you threaten to leave again; yet you know I built this house for the two of you so I'd get to see you at least in the summer. And when a person is as old as I, he needs to live for others.

SON: Huh! You're not old! Today people could think you were out courting with a rose in your buttonhole.

FATHER: There *is* a limit, *even* in joking! What do you think, Kerstin?

DAUGHTER-IN-LAW: Oh, Knut is terrible, and if I didn't know he means nothing by what he says . . .

FATHER: If he doesn't mean anything by what he says, he's an idiot! (*Observes an unfinished portrait of the* FRIEND.) Who is this supposed to be?

SON: Can't you see it's the friend—of the family.

FATHER: What a mean expression—he looks as if he were an evil person—in this portrait!

DAUGHTER-IN-LAW: Yes, but he isn't!

FATHER: A person without religion is evil, and a man who has broken up his marriage is evil.

DAUGHTER-IN-LAW: But he didn't break his marriage, he had a court do that.

FATHER: There was a time when Knut always spoke unfavorably about your friend. How come he's so taken with him now?

SON: I didn't really know him, but I've learned to. Have you got rid of all your morning complaining?

FATHER: Have you heard this saying?

SON: I've heard all your sayings and all your anecdotes!

FATHER: There is a time for love—there is a time for hate! Good-bye! (*Goes.*)

DAUGHTER-IN-LAW (*to the* COUSIN *who is about to water the flowers*): I've watered the flowers, my friend!

COUSIN: Don't call me your friend—you don't mean it—you hate me!

DAUGHTER-IN-LAW: I don't hate you, even though you cause all the dissension in the family!

SON: There! Now you two are at it, too!

DAUGHTER-IN-LAW: If I could only detect any good intentions in Adele's attentions to my house, but there's always reproach and criticism in her way of doing me a favor.

COUSIN: That's how you feel because you neglect your house and your child, but I have only one purpose in everything I do and say, and that's to be useful so that I don't have to feel I'm living on charity! But you! You!

SON (*approaches the* COUSIN *and studies her*): So you do have temperament? Then you have passions, too!

DAUGHTER-IN-LAW: How do her passions concern you?

COUSIN: Well, anyone who's poor mayn't have any likes, any opinions, any passions! But anyone who marries wealth, gets what she wants, has the table set and the bed made up for her and lives as she wants to, day—and night!

DAUGHTER-IN-LAW: Haven't you any shame?

COUSIN: But watch out for me, you! I can see and I can hear, too! (*Goes.*)

SON: I think all hell's loose today!

DAUGHTER-IN-LAW: Not yet, but it can be! Watch out for that girl! Have you thought of the possibility your mother could die?

SON: Well, what then?

DAUGHTER-IN-LAW: Then your father could remarry!

SON: With Adele?

DAUGHTER-IN-LAW: Yes!

SON: Ah! I suppose one could prevent that as far as that goes . . . That would mean she'd be my stepmother and her children would share the inheritance!

DAUGHTER-IN-LAW: They say your father has already provided for Adele in his will!

SON: What do you think about their relationship?

DAUGHTER-IN-LAW: Everything! And nothing! This much is certain: He's in love with the girl!

SON: In love! Maybe! But nothing more!

DAUGHTER-IN-LAW: So much so he was jealous of Axel last summer!

SON: Well, can't we get the two young ones to marry?

DAUGHTER-IN-LAW: Axel isn't caught that easily!

SON: He's as inflammable as all widowers!

DAUGHTER-IN-LAW: Yes, but he's to be pitied . . . he's too good for a demon like that.

SON: I don't know what's wrong this year, but the air has gotten close. It's as if a storm were building up, and I get a damnably strong longing to go away.

DAUGHTER-IN-LAW: Yes, but you can't sell any paintings, can you? And if we go, your father will cut off our allowance! Let's talk with Axel about all this—he has a gift for straightening out things for others, though he can't for himself.

SON: I don't know that it's wise to let outsiders in on family squabbles . . .

DAUGHTER-IN-LAW: Do you call our only friend an outsider . . .

SON: Yes, be that as it may, but family is family . . . besides . . . I don't know . . . the old man used to say: Always treat your friends as if they could become your enemies . . .

DAUGHTER-IN-LAW: So you're quoting the old man's sayings now. He also has a despicable saying: Fear the one you love.

SON: Yes, he can be too severe when he wants to!

DAUGHTER-IN-LAW (*Looking out. The* FRIEND, *dressed in light summer costume with a blue scarf and white tennis shoes, enters*): Well, at last! (*Going up to Axel*) Good morning, sleepyhead!

SON: Good morning to you!

FRIEND: Good morning, good friends! I suppose you've been waiting for me?

DAUGHTER-IN-LAW: Yes, indeed!

SON: My wife has been absolutely upset because you didn't get any sleep last night!

FRIEND (*embarrassed*): How's that? How's that?

SON (*to his wife*): Look, he's bashful! (*The* DAUGHTER-IN-LAW *stares at the* FRIEND *with curiosity.*)

FRIEND: It's a wonderful morning, and when I've slept under two happy people's roof, life can still smile at me!

SON: You think we're rather happy?

FRIEND: Yes, and the one who's doubly happy is your father, who can *re*live a pleasant life with his own children and grandchildren. Few people get an old age like that.

SON: Don't envy anyone!

FRIEND: I don't, quite the opposite: I'm delighted by seeing how life can be beautiful for some people . . . because that gives me the hope it could turn out brighter for me in the future. And especially when I consider what a painful life your father has lived through—financial failure, exile, getting thrown out of his own family . . .

SON: And now he has a house and possessions, his son well married—right?

FRIEND: Yes, there can't be any doubt of that!

SON: Listen: You were in love with my wife last year, weren't you?

FRIEND: No, I won't say that, though I certainly showed I was fond of her . . . but I'm over that now!

DAUGHTER-IN-LAW: You're certainly fickle!

FRIEND: Yes, in my infatuations! Fortunately—for me!

SON: But why did you rush off last summer? Was it because of that other woman; or perhaps because of Adele?

FRIEND (*embarrassed*): Your questions are getting too personal.

SON: It was Adele! See, Kerstin!

DAUGHTER-IN-LAW: He didn't have to be afraid of her!

FRIEND: I'm not afraid of the ladies, but of my feelings for the ladies!

SON: You have an exceptional talent for shifting so one can't ever know about you.

FRIEND: Why should you want to know about me any more than about anyone else?

SON: Do you know what my father said about your portrait?

DAUGHTER-IN-LAW: Knut!

SON: He said it looked like an evil person.

FRIEND: Maybe it's like the original—just now I'm really very bad—for the moment.

DAUGHTER-IN-LAW: You're always bragging about your being bad . . .

FRIEND: Probably to conceal it?

DAUGHTER-IN-LAW: No, you're a good human being, much

better than you want to be. But you shouldn't frighten
your friends away . . .

FRIEND: Are you afraid of me?

DAUGHTER-IN-LAW: Yes, sometimes, when I can't
understand you!

SON: You should get married again; that's the whole trouble.

FRIEND: The whole trouble! And with whom?

SON: With Adele, for example!

FRIEND: Please don't talk about that.

SON: See, there we have the sore point! So it was Adele all
the same.

FRIEND: Listen, friends, maybe I should put on a black coat
. . .

DAUGHTER-IN-LAW: Don't change your clothes—what you
have on is absolutely charming, and Adele will be
delighted.

SON: Did you hear that? My wife thinks you're charming!

DAUGHTER-IN-LAW: Is it so dangerous to say how becoming
clothes are?

SON: It's a little unusual at least for a woman to say such
polite things to a man! But then we're unusual people.

FRIEND: Will the two of you go with me to look for rooms
later?

DAUGHTER-IN-LAW: What? Don't you intend to stay with us?

FRIEND: No, that was never my intention!

SON: There, you see!

DAUGHTER-IN-LAW: Why don't you want to stay with us?
Why?

FRIEND: I don't know . . . I think you two need some privacy
. . . and it could happen we'd get tired of each other.

DAUGHTER-IN-LAW: Are you already tired of us! Listen, it
just won't do for you to live anywhere else for people will
start talking . . .

FRIEND: Talking? About what?

DAUGHTER-IN-LAW: Ah! You know how they concoct stories . . .

SON: You stay right here, quite simply! Let them talk! If you stay here, you're my wife's lover, of course, and, if you stay in town, we've broken off our friendship, or I've thrown you out! So it's more flattering for you to be considered my wife's lover, it seems to me. Right?

FRIEND: You speak rather bluntly, but I prefer to do what's more flattering for the two of you.

DAUGHTER-IN-LAW: You *do* have a secret reason you don't want to tell us.

FRIEND: Frankly . . . I don't dare! Yes yes, yes yes! A person gets so used to other people's lives so easily, enjoys their happiness so that at last one weaves one's feelings into others'; and then it's hard to part.

SON: Why should we part? Look, you're living here: offer my wife your arm and we'll go take a walk. (*The* FRIEND *offers the* DAUGHTER-IN-LAW *his arm somewhat embarrassed.*)

DAUGHTER-IN-LAW: Why, I think you're trembling! He's trembling, Knut!

SON: See, how nicely you walk together! But he's really trembling! Stay home if you're freezing!

FRIEND: If you permit, I'll sit here reading the papers.

DAUGHTER-IN-LAW: Gladly, and I'll send Adele in to keep you company! We'll just go out to do a little shopping, Knut and I! (*Waves to* ADELE *who is outside.*) Come here, Adele, and you'll get something! [ADELE *enters.*]

FRIEND: Won't you keep me company while husband and wife go out shopping?

COUSIN: Company? Are you afraid of the dark?

FRIEND: Yes, very much! (*The* SON *and the* DAUGHTER-IN-LAW *go. The* FRIEND *looks to see they are gone.*) I don't want to miss the chance to speak confidentially with you as a relative of theirs! May I?

COUSIN: Go ahead!

FRIEND: You know how much I like the two . . . you smile, and I know what you mean. It's true Kerstin as a young woman does have appeal, but I assure you I control my feelings, that only for a moment did I fear losing my control.

COUSIN: That you're attracted a little to Kerstin doesn't amaze me—I know her ability to charm people, but your finding Knut's company attractive I don't understand. Why, he's an insignificant man, far inferior to you both in talent and experience . . .

FRIEND: Completely childish, you mean, but that's just what comforts me after associating with intellectuals all winter . . .

COUSIN: Playing with children is comforting but can become boring, yet you never get tired of Knut. Why don't you?

FRIEND: I haven't thought about it, but you seem to have. What do you think?

COUSIN: That you, without knowing it, are in love with Kerstin.

FRIEND: I don't think so; rather I love the two of them together so I don't find the same pleasure in the company of one as in that of both when they're together. Seeing them separately would put both of them at a distance from me. But assume that you'd be right in saying I'm infatuated with Kerstin. What difference would that make as long as I conceal my feelings?

COUSIN: Feelings have a way of making themselves known, and fire spreads.

FRIEND: Maybe, but there still doesn't seem to be any danger. Be sure that I after going through all the agonies of divorce would never witness another or be the cause of it. Besides . . . Kerstin loves her husband . . .

COUSIN: Loves? She never has, and their love is merely a

quiet marital liking. But Knut has a passionate nature that's going to weary of wild strawberries and milk . . .

FRIEND: Listen, you *have* been engaged!

COUSIN: How so?

FRIEND: You sound like an expert! So I'll go deeper! A lot has changed here since last year!

COUSIN: What?

FRIEND: There's another atmosphere, another way of talking and thinking . . . there's something that disturbs me!

COUSIN: You've noticed! Well, it's a strange family! The father a man of independent means without anything to do for the last ten years; the son born a person of independent means. They eat, they sleep, and wait for their deaths, killing time in the most pleasant ways possible. No purpose in life, no ambition, no passions, but a lot out of Solomon's proverbs. Have you noticed a certain saying comes up every other hour in this house: "He's a bad human being!" is served as bread for everything.

FRIEND: How wonderfully well you speak. And what a keen observer!

COUSIN: As keenly as hate! Yes!

FRIEND: A person who hates like you must also be able to love!

COUSIN: Hm!

FRIEND: Adele, now that we've said nasty things about our friends, we must be friends ourselves, whether we want to or not—

COUSIN: Whether we want to or not!

FRIEND: Shake hands on that! But promise you won't hate—me.

COUSIN (*shakes his hands*): Your hands are cold. (*The* DAUGHTER-IN-LAW *appears in the doorway for a moment.*)

FRIEND: But you're all the warmer!

COUSIN: Sh-h! There's Kerstin!

FRIEND: Then we'll have to continue this conversation another time . . .

[*The* DAUGHTER-IN-LAW *comes up to them. Silence.*]

DAUGHTER-IN-LAW: How quiet you got? Am I interrupting?

COUSIN: Not at all! I'm probably the one who's interrupting!

DAUGHTER-IN-LAW (*gives the* FRIEND *a letter*): Here's a letter for you! I see it's from a woman! (*The* FRIEND *looks at the letter and turns pale.*) How pale you turned! If you're still freezing, you may borrow my shawl! (*She takes off her shawl and puts it over his shoulders.*)

FRIEND: Thanks! At least that's warm!

COUSIN: Maybe you ought to have a pillow under your feet.

DAUGHTER-IN-LAW: It'd be better if you told them to build a fire up in his room, for there's dampness from the sea if it has rained for a few days.

COUSIN: Yes, you're right about that!

FRIEND: Don't go to so much trouble for me! Don't!

COUSIN: Oh, it's no trouble! (*Silence. Goes.*)

FRIEND: How quiet it got!

DAUGHTER-IN-LAW: Just as it did a minute ago! What were you up to? Secrets?

FRIEND: I pitied myself a little—one doesn't grow away from that.

DAUGHTER-IN-LAW: Pity yourself a little to me! You're unhappy . . .

FRIEND: Mainly because I can't work.

DAUGHTER-IN-LAW: And you can't work because . . .

FRIEND: Because?

DAUGHTER-IN-LAW: Are you still in love with your wife?

FRIEND: No, not with her, but with my memory of her.

DAUGHTER-IN-LAW: Recall your memories then!

FRIEND: Never!

DAUGHTER-IN-LAW: Was she the one you ran away to last fall?

FRIEND: No, it wasn't! But to others! Since you ask.

DAUGHTER-IN-LAW: Shame!

FRIEND: Yes, when the horseflies sting it's a comfort to roll in the dirt; it makes the skin hard.

DAUGHTER-IN-LAW: Shame! You!

FRIEND: Besides there's legal dirt and . . . illegal.

DAUGHTER-IN-LAW: What do you mean?

FRIEND: You're married, and we're not confirmands—so: I mean in marriage one rests as if in consecrated ground, but outside marriage in unconsecrated. But it's dirt, all the same!

DAUGHTER-IN-LAW: Surely you wouldn't compare . . .

FRIEND: Yes, I would compare . . .

DAUGHTER-IN-LAW: What sort of woman were you married to, really?

FRIEND: A respectable girl from a very good family!

DAUGHTER-IN-LAW: And you loved her?

FRIEND: All too much!

DAUGHTER-IN-LAW: And then?

FRIEND: We hated each other.

DAUGHTER-IN-LAW: But why? Why?

FRIEND: That's one of the many unanswered questions in life!

DAUGHTER-IN-LAW: But there has to be a reason!

FRIEND: I thought so, too, but the reasons turned out to be consequences of our hatred. Our quarrels didn't bring about our breaking up, but when love died, our quarrels started. That's why the so-called loveless marriages are the happy ones.

DAUGHTER-IN-LAW (*naïvely*): Yes, we really never have any serious unpleasantness, Knut and I.

FRIEND: Now you were too frank, Kerstin!

DAUGHTER-IN-LAW: Why, what did I say?

FRIEND: You said you've never loved your husband!

DAUGHTER-IN-LAW: Loved? Well! What is loving?

FRIEND (*gets up*): What a question, from a married woman! What love is? Well, it is one of the things one does, but can't put into words.

DAUGHTER-IN-LAW: Was your wife pretty?

FRIEND: Yes, I thought so. She looked like you, as far as that goes.

DAUGHTER-IN-LAW: Do you think I'm pretty?

FRIEND: Yes!

DAUGHTER-IN-LAW: My husband didn't think so until you told him, and it's funny how attached to me he is if only you're here. It's as if your presence set him on fire!

FRIEND: Really! And that's why he likes to have me here. How about you?

DAUGHTER-IN-LAW: I?

FRIEND: Maybe one ought to stop now before we go too far.

DAUGHTER-IN-LAW (*angry*): What do you mean? What are you thinking about me?

FRIEND: Nothing bad, Kerstin! Nothing! Forgive me if I've hurt you!

DAUGHTER-IN-LAW: You've hurt me terribly! But I know what a low opinion you have of women.

FRIEND: Not about all of them! To me you are . . .

DAUGHTER-IN-LAW: What?

FRIEND: My friend's wife, and therefore . . .

DAUGHTER-IN-LAW: And if I weren't?

FRIEND: Shall we stop? Kerstin, it seems to me you're not used to attentions from men—

DAUGHTER-IN-LAW: I'm not. That's why I appreciate being liked! Just a little!

FRIEND: Just a little! You certainly have the qualifications for happiness with such small demands on life.

DAUGHTER-IN-LAW: What do you know about my demands?

FRIEND: Are you ambitious? Would you possibly try to get out, get up, become something?

DAUGHTER-IN-LAW: No! Nothing like that! But this monotonous life, without work, without excitement, without anything ever happening! You know I get so grim occasionally I wish I'd get a great sorrow, that a plague, a fire would strike (*whispers*), that my child would die! That I would die myself!

FRIEND: Do you know what's wrong? Idleness, too much earthly bliss, probably something else.

DAUGHTER-IN-LAW: What?

FRIEND: Lust!

DAUGHTER-IN-LAW: What did you say?

FRIEND: I don't need to repeat the word, especially since I think you heard it; but since I don't give it any nasty meaning, I don't think I've insulted you!

DAUGHTER-IN-LAW: You're certainly unlike everybody else—you hit your friends in the face without their really feeling it!

FRIEND: And they say there are women who like to be hit.

DAUGHTER-IN-LAW: Now you make me afraid of you!

FRIEND: Fine!

DAUGHTER-IN-LAW: Who are you? What do you want? What are your intentions?

FRIEND: Don't be curious about me, Kerstin!

DAUGHTER-IN-LAW: Still another bit of impertinence!

FRIEND: A bit of friendly advice! It suggests your need of a safety valve!

DAUGHTER-IN-LAW: Sometimes I feel I could hate you.

FRIEND: That's a good sign! But haven't you ever felt you could love me?

DAUGHTER-IN-LAW: Yes, sometimes.

FRIEND: Tell me when!

DAUGHTER-IN-LAW: I really feel like answering your frankness . . . Well, when you're talking with Adele!

FRIEND: That's a striking reminder of your husband's fire,

which always flames up for you, when I'm present. Adele and I seem to have the function of getting the fire started.

DAUGHTER-IN-LAW (*laughs*): That sounded so funny, I can't get angry.

FRIEND: You should never get angry—it's less becoming to you than to others. But to change the subject. Where is your husband? (*Gets up, looks out of the window. The* DAUGHTER-IN-LAW *joins him.*) I didn't intend to call your attention to what's happening down there in the garden . . .

DAUGHTER-IN-LAW: As if I hadn't seen Knut kiss Adele before.

FRIEND: But that Adele can't turn on your husband for you disturbs me. There are a lot of things in this house that disturb me this year! You know, there's certainly something rotting here!

DAUGHTER-IN-LAW: How so? I can't see it! It's only a game as far as that goes.

FRIEND: Yes, there's playing with fire, hunting knives, and dynamite sticks! I think it's ghastly!

FATHER (*enters, wearing his hat*): Is Knut here?

DAUGHTER-IN-LAW: No, he went out shopping! Did you want to see him?

FATHER: Yes, since I'm asking about him! Have you seen Adele?

DAUGHTER-IN-LAW: Not for quite a while.

FATHER (*notices the* FRIEND): Excuse me, I didn't see you! How are you?

FRIEND: Fine, thank you! And how are you, sir?

DAUGHTER-IN-LAW: Can I do anything?

FATHER: Yes, if you would! But I'm probably disturbing—I can come back.

DAUGHTER-IN-LAW: You're not . . .

FATHER: The thing is this: there are mosquitoes in my bedroom so I thought I'd ask if I could sleep in your attic.

DAUGHTER-IN-LAW: Too bad, we've just given Axel that room!

FATHER: Oh, he's going to stay here! If I'd known, I would never have suggested . . .

FRIEND: I'd never have accepted their offer to stay here if I'd know that you, sir . . .

FATHER: Don't mention it, I'm not going to be in the way, and it's not good to be between the bark and the tree! (*Silence.*) Has Knut started painting yet?

DAUGHTER-IN-LAW: No, he's not in the mood!

FATHER: He has never been in the mood to work, and still less now.

DAUGHTER-IN-LAW: Was there anything else?

FATHER: No! It doesn't matter! Well, you don't have to say anything to Knut about the room.

DAUGHTER-IN-LAW: I'll be delighted not to mention it!

FATHER: You understand, it's not at all pleasant to stir up dissension—in vain. It would have been different if the room had been available, and I could really have had it, but now that it's taken . . . Well, good-bye! (*Leaves.*)

FRIEND: Excuse me, Kerstin, for leaving you for a little while!

DAUGHTER-IN-LAW: Where are you going—in such a hurry?

FRIEND: That—I can't tell you!

DAUGHTER-IN-LAW: You're going out to rent a room! You mustn't!

FRIEND (*has picked up his hat*): Do you think I'd stay in your house after being told to get out like that?

DAUGHTER-IN-LAW (*tries to take his hat*): No, you mustn't go! We're not the ones who told you. Besides . . .

SON (*enters*): What now! Are you fighting? Or is it a declaration of love?

DAUGHTER-IN-LAW: It's only friendly bickering, but can you imagine that restless Axel wants to go out to rent a room because Father came in and wanted the attic room?

SON: Did he want the attic room? He wanted to see what you were up to, of course! And so you're thinking of leaving. Get down on your knees and ask her forgiveness! (*The* FRIEND *kneels.*) Kiss her foot! She has beautiful feet!

FRIEND (*kisses her foot, then gets up*): Well, now I've asked for forgiveness for going out to rent a room! Good-bye for a while! (*Leaves hastily.*)

DAUGHTER-IN-LAW (*irritated*): Axel! I think it really was indecent of the old man to interfere like this and disturb us! Now we won't have a minute's peace, night or day.

SON: We'll have to put up with that! But you could try to conceal your feelings, a little bit!

DAUGHTER-IN-LAW: What feelings? What do you mean? Maybe you are—jealous?

SON: What? Now I don't know what's what! I'm talking about your feeling of resentment toward Father!

DAUGHTER-IN-LAW (*changing her manner*): We won't talk about feelings any more! Put on this tie so you'll look like a human being. (*She takes a package out of her pocket.*)

SON: Am I to have a tie again? And a blue one at that!

DAUGHTER-IN-LAW (*tying a blue tie on* KNUT): You're not to wear dirty clothes either! And straighten the ends of your moustache . . .

SON: You know what? You're entirely too obvious!

DAUGHTER-IN-LAW: What?

SON: Maybe I ought to get light clothes, too, and tennis shoes.

DAUGHTER-IN-LAW: Yes, you'd look good in them—you're getting fat.

SON: And I should lose some weight! And be a little haggard! And be divorced, too?

DAUGHTER-IN-LAW: Knut, you are jealous!

SON: Maybe gone beyond the limit? But how strange! I'm jealous without envy or anger. I like the man so much I could deny him nothing! Nothing!

DAUGHTER-IN-LAW: Nothing! That's saying a lot!

SON: Yes, that's how it is! It's crazy, criminal, low, but if he asked if he could sleep with you, I'd let him!

DAUGHTER-IN-LAW: Now you're absolutely terrible. I've heard a lot from that mouth of yours, and I've had to . . .

SON: I can't help it's like this! You know, I'm sometimes pursued by a vision, both when I'm awake and when I'm sleeping: I think I see you two together, and it doesn't hurt me; rather I enjoy it as at the sight of something very beautiful!

DAUGHTER-IN-LAW: But that's beyond belief!

SON: Maybe it is unusual, but admit it's damnably interesting!

DAUGHTER-IN-LAW: Sometimes I think you want to get rid of me!

SON: You don't believe that!

DAUGHTER-IN-LAW: Yes, sometimes! It seems to me as if you were shoving Axel at me so you'd get us together, get a case against me, and could divorce me!

SON: This is unbelievable! Tell me, Kerstin: Haven't you two kissed each other?

DAUGHTER-IN-LAW: By all that's sacred, no!

SON: Promise me that when you do you'll tell me right to my face: That's how it is.

DAUGHTER-IN-LAW: Listen, Knut, don't go crazy!

SON: Exactly! You see, I don't want to be deceived. I won't give you up willingly, but still rather that.

DAUGHTER-IN-LAW: If you'll stop your sermon, I'll start mine! What are your relations with Adele?

SON: Just what you know about and approve!

DAUGHTER-IN-LAW: I've never approved adultery!

SON: There, that's your tune now! What was innocent a while ago is a crime now!

DAUGHTER-IN-LAW: Exactly as my absolutely innocent relationship with Axel a while ago!

SON: It's innocent today, but who knows what it will be tomorrow!

DAUGHTER-IN-LAW: Wait till tomorrow then!

SON: No, I don't want to wait until it's too late!

DAUGHTER-IN-LAW: What do you want?

SON: I don't know! Yes, an end to this! If there is any! We've woven the nets ourselves, and now we're caught! Oh, how I hate him when he isn't here. But the minute I see him and he looks at me with his big eyes, I love him like a brother, a sister . . . I understand now how you can be under his influence! But I don't quite understand myself. It seems to me I've gone here alone among women until my feelings have turned feminine and as if your love for him must have infected me. You must love him terribly, though you don't know it!

DAUGHTER-IN-LAW: That's right! And now you only want to blame someone else!

SON: Just as you do!

DAUGHTER-IN-LAW: As you!

SON: As you! Now I'll go crazy!

DAUGHTER-IN-LAW: I don't doubt it!

SON: And you don't feel sorry for me!

DAUGHTER-IN-LAW: Should I feel sorry for you when you torture me?

SON: You have never loved me!

DAUGHTER-IN-LAW: You've never loved me!

SON: Well, we got into what'll last until we die!

DAUGHTER-IN-LAW: Let's stop in time! Go take a dip in the sea—that'll cool you off!

SON: You want to be alone! (*The* FRIEND *comes in.*)

FRIEND (*openly and happily*): Well, I really have had luck! Just as I was going, I met Adele who had a room . . .

DAUGHTER-IN-LAW: Does she have rooms to rent, too?

FRIEND: She knew of a room!

DAUGHTER-IN-LAW: She certainly knows everything, that girl!

FRIEND (*to the* SON, *offering him a cigarette case*): A cigarette?

SON (*sharply*): No, thanks!

FRIEND: That's a nice tie!

SON: You think so?

FRIEND: You've been talking about me while I was gone! I can tell!

SON (*irritated*): Excuse me! I have to go take a dip! (*Leaves hastily.*)

FRIEND: What's wrong with him?

DAUGHTER-IN-LAW: He's jealous!

FRIEND: Really! But he hasn't any excuse.

DAUGHTER-IN-LAW: Knut insists he has! Where did Adele have that room you were talking about?

FRIEND (*absentmindedly*): Adele? Oh, right across the street at the pilot's!

DAUGHTER-IN-LAW: That's nicely figured out. Then you can look right into her room! What a schemer!

FRIEND: I don't think Adele ever thought of that.

DAUGHTER-IN-LAW: Adele? Have you become that intimate?

FRIEND: Don't summon up ghosts that could rouse feelings which wouldn't otherwise show up in broad daylight. Don't do it, or . . .

DAUGHTER-IN-LAW: You'll go away as usual. But you mayn't now; you don't have the right.

FRIEND (*lights a cigarette*): Perhaps the duty!

DAUGHTER-IN-LAW: If you're my friend, you'll not leave me defenseless in this house where my honor's threatened! Where my offending husband under his parents'

protection can stoop to the lowest meanness! Imagine if
you can—he's so far gone in depravity he'd turn me over to
you—if necessary!

FRIEND: That's a charming form of jealousy! And what did
you say to that?

DAUGHTER-IN-LAW: What should I have said?

FRIEND: You ask me!

DAUGHTER-IN-LAW (*hysterically*): You're playing like a cat
with his prey! You see how I'm caught in your web, how
I'm suffering and fighting to get free, but I can't! Be kind,
give me one friendly look and don't sit there like an
unfeeling statue who's expecting adoration and sacrifice.
(*She falls to her knees.*) You're so strong you can control
your emotions, so proud, so honorable, but that's because
you have never loved anyone, never loved as I love you!

FRIEND: Haven't I? Get up, Kerstin! And sit down way over
there in the easy chair! Like that! Now I'm going to have
my say! (*He remains sitting with his cigarette in his hand.*) I
have loved you—as they say—from the first moment I saw
you. Remember the sunset when we first met last year?
Your husband was standing painting down in the valley
when I went by. I was presented to you, and we stood
there talking until we got tired and you sat down in the
grass and asked me to sit down beside you. But the dew
was heavy, and I didn't want to get wet. You unbuttoned
your coat and told me to sit on it. That seemed to me as if
you had opened your arms and asked me to rest in your
embrace. I was very unhappy, very tired and forlorn, and it
looked very warm and soft inside your coat. I really wanted
to crawl in and hide by your young, virginal bosom, but I
felt ashamed when I saw in your innocent eyes a faint smile
because a man like me could be embarrassed! We met
again, again and again! Your husband seemed to enjoy my

admiration of you; it looked as if I had discovered his wife for him. I became your captive, and you played with me; your husband didn't hesitate to tease me about it even in large gatherings. His conceit and his cocksureness hurt me at times, and there were moments when I was tempted to push him aside and try to take his place. Do you remember the afternoon when I had invited you both over on my birthday? You were going to come later. And when we had waited for an hour, you came in dressed in a purple skirt with a light flowered blouse; you had a wide brimmed hat covered by yellow voile which cast golden sunlight over your whole figure. And when you handed me a bouquet of roses with a fourteen-year-old girl's shy daring, I thought you were so devastatingly beautiful I couldn't speak, either to say "Welcome" or "Thank you" for the flowers, but I went out and wept!

DAUGHTER-IN-LAW: At least you can conceal your feelings!

FRIEND: Do you remember later that night, after supper when we had exchanged reminiscenses and embraced each other's souls, how Knut formally, and apparently with your consent, invited me to live in your home in town during the winter? Do you remember what I answered?

DAUGHTER-IN-LAW: You said: I don't dare!

FRIEND: The next morning I was gone!

DAUGHTER-IN-LAW: And I wept all that day! And Knut wept, too!

FRIEND: Imagine how much weeping we'll get done now!

DAUGHTER-IN-LAW: Now?

FRIEND: Sit still. Now that we've said everything, all that's left for us is to part!

DAUGHTER-IN-LAW: No! No! Not part! Why can't it stay the way it is? You're so calm, and I'm not at all uneasy! What does Knut have to do with our feelings as long as we

control them? Why, we're sitting here calmly talking things
over just like an old married couple talking about how they
loved each other when they were young.

FRIEND: Child! I don't understand how you've been married
when you can believe in friendship after a declaration of
love! I'm as calm as a powder keg under a detonator; I'm as
cool as a fired-up furnace—oh! I've fought, I've tortured
myself, but I can't answer for myself.

DAUGHTER-IN-LAW: But I can answer for myself!

FRIEND: Yes, I can believe that—you put out the fire
whenever it flames up, but I live alone! Oh, what a
damnable thought! And you think I'll be willing to live in
this house on crumbs from the rich man's table, gulp down
air, drink the fragrance of flowers, and go about with pangs
of conscience anyway?

DAUGHTER-IN-LAW: Why should you have pangs of
conscience when *he* doesn't hold himself too good to
have a lover that he kisses!

FRIEND: Let's not blame anyone else. If we do, we're on the
edge and then all that's left is to jump into the sea! No,
let's be different for once; let's show the world an example
of decent human beings. We'll tell Knut the minute he
comes in: This is how it is, we love each other; tell us what
we should do!

DAUGHTER-IN-LAW: Great! Wonderful! Yes, we'll do that,
come what may! And we can do it honestly for we haven't
done anything wrong!

FRIEND: And then? He'll ask me to leave, of course!

DAUGHTER-IN-LAW: Or to stay!

FRIEND: On what condition? That everything remains as it
was? No, I can't! Do you think I could stand seeing you
caress each other, shut your bedroom door in the evening
. . . No! There's no end to this! But he has to know;

otherwise, I'll never be able to look him in the eye, never shake his hand! We must tell him everything—then we'll see!

DAUGHTER-IN-LAW: If that were only over! Tell me you love me; otherwise I'll not have the courage to plunge the knife in his back! Tell me you love me!

FRIEND (*they remain seated*): I love you, body and soul; I love your little feet I can see under the hem of your dress; I love your little, white teeth and your kissable mouth, your ears and your sensuously friendly eyes—I love your whole light, airy figure that I'd like to throw on my shoulder and run into the forest with! When I was young, I once took a girl in my arms on the street and ran up four flights with her—I was young then; imagine, now when I'm grownup!

DAUGHTER-IN-LAW: Love my soul, too!

FRIEND: I love your soul since it's weaker than mine, fiery like mine, faithless like mine . . .

DAUGHTER-IN-LAW: Mayn't I get up and go to you now?

FRIEND: No! You mayn't!

DAUGHTER-IN-LAW: Knut's coming, I hear him, and I won't have the courage to tell him before I've kissed your forehead.

FRIEND: Is he coming?

DAUGHTER-IN-LAW: Sh-h!

(*The* FATHER *enters, wearing his hat, and goes right up to the* FRIEND, *who is visibly startled and gets up.*)

FATHER (*picks up a newspaper on a table back of the* FRIEND): Excuse me, I was only going to get a paper. (*To the* DAUGHTER-IN-LAW) Have you seen Adele?

DAUGHTER-IN-LAW: That's the fifth time you ask about Adele!

FATHER: Have you been keeping count? Aren't you going to take a dip before breakfast?

DAUGHTER-IN-LAW: No! Not today!

FATHER: It isn't right to neglect the baths when your health is delicate.

(*Silence. The* FATHER *goes.*)

FRIEND: No, I can't stay here any longer! I can't take it!

DAUGHTER-IN-LAW (*comes up to him and observes him with excitement*): Shall we run away?

FRIEND: No! But I'm going to!

DAUGHTER-IN-LAW: Then I'll run away, too! Then we'll die together!

FRIEND (*embraces and kisses her*): Now we're lost! Why did I do this? An end to honor and faith, to friendship and peace! Fire from Hell that burns and scorches everything that was green and blooming! (*They separate to go to sit down apart. The* SON *enters, hastily.*)

SON: Why are you sitting so far apart?

DAUGHTER-IN-LAW: Because . . .

SON: And look so stirred up!

DAUGHTER-IN-LAW: Because . . . (*a long pause*) we love each other!

SON (*looks at both of them for a while, then to the* FRIEND): Is that true?

FRIEND: It's true!

SON (*sits down on a chair, somewhat crushed*): Why did you have to tell me?

DAUGHTER-IN-LAW: That's what one gets for being decent!

SON: It's very different, but it is shameless!

DAUGHTER-IN-LAW: But you asked me when the time came . . .

SON: That's true! And the time has come. It seems to me I already knew it; yet it's still so new I can't grasp it. Whose fault is it? No one's and everyone's! What shall we do? What's going to happen?

FRIEND: Do you have any criticism of my conduct?

SON: None! You fled when you saw the danger; you turned down our invitation to stay with us; you concealed your feelings so that Kerstin thought you hated her. But why did you come back?

FRIEND: Because I thought my feelings were dead!

SON: That's likely, and I believe you! But we're facing a fact which we've not caused or managed to prevent; we tried to avoid the danger by artificial openness, joked about it, but the danger's come closer and closer and now has hit us. What are we going to do now? Let's talk calmly and try to remain friends! What's to be done? (*Silence.*) No one answers! But we can't sit here seeing how the fire's broken out without doing something! (*Gets up.*) Let's think about the consequences!

FRIEND: Wouldn't it be best if I withdrew?

SON: I think so!

DAUGHTER-IN-LAW (*wildly*): No, you mustn't go! I'll follow you!

SON: Is that talking calmly?

DAUGHTER-IN-LAW: Love isn't calm! (*Approaches the* FRIEND.)

SON: At least spare me the sight of your lust! Spare my feelings a little—I'm relatively innocent and will be the one who suffers.

DAUGHTER-IN-LAW (*puts her arm about the* FRIEND): You may not go!

SON (*takes his wife by the arm and draws her away from the* FRIEND): You can at least behave decently until I've gone out! (*To the* FRIEND) Listen, my friend! We have to settle this in a hurry, for the breakfast bell will ring in a few minutes. I see you can't overcome your love, which I could with a little effort. To continue living with a woman who loves another man can't be satisfactory to me since I'd always feel I was living in polyandry. So—I'll give way—but not before I have a guarantee you'll marry her.

FRIEND: I don't know why, but your nobleminded offer humiliates me more than my feeling of guilt if I had stolen her.

SON: I imagine, but it humiliates me less if I give than if you steal. I'll give you five minutes to settle this. So, good-bye for a moment! (*Goes.*)

DAUGHTER-IN-LAW: Well-l?

FRIEND: Don't you see I'm ridiculous?

DAUGHTER-IN-LAW: No! It isn't ridiculous to be decent!

FRIEND: Not always, but in this case the husband seems to be least ridiculous! And you'll get to despise me some day!

DAUGHTER-IN-LAW: Is this all you have to say to me at a moment like this? Now when there's nothing in the way and you could open your arms with a clear conscience . . . you hesitate!

FRIEND: Yes, I'm hesitating, because this openness is taking on the appearance of pure impudence, this decency of heartlessness . . .

DAUGHTER-IN-LAW: There! There!

FRIEND: And I think that that smell of rottenness which I noticed in this house comes from you!

DAUGHTER-IN-LAW: Or from you! You were the one who seduced me with your bashful glances, with your pretended coolness, with your brutalities which stirred me up like a whip! And now the seducer's playing the role of the righteous one!—

FRIEND: Or like this: You were the one . . .

DAUGHTER-IN-LAW: No, it was you, you, you! (*She throws herself down on the sofa and screams.*) Help me then! I'm dying! I'm dying! (*The* FRIEND *stands absolutely still.*) Can't you help me? Haven't you any mercy? You're an animal! Don't you see I'm sick? Help me! Help me! Get a doctor! At least do me the favor any human being would do for a stranger! Call Adele! (*The* FRIEND *goes. Then the* SON *enters.*)

SON: Well-l? What's wrong? Didn't you come to an agreement?

DAUGHTER-IN-LAW Sh-h! Not another word!

SON: But why did he take off in such a hurry through the garden? I thought he'd take the bushes and trees with him and it almost looked as if he had fire in his pants!

(*The* MOTHER *and the* COUSIN *enter.*)

MOTHER: Won't you come to breakfast now?

SON: Yes, thank you, that would really suit us.

MOTHER: But where's Axel? Shall we wait for him or not?

SON: We won't wait for him at all, for he has taken off!

MOTHER: He's certainly a queer man! And I've cooked the flounders! . . .

(*The* FATHER *enters.*)

SON (*to the* FATHER): Now you may have the room if you want it!

FATHER: Thank you, but now I don't need it!

SON: You certainly change your mind!

FATHER: Others, too, I suspect! But the one who controls his heart is better than the one who wins cities!

SON: And there's this one: Do not say to your friend, go away and come back.

FATHER: That is very good! Where did you get it?

SON: I got it from Kerstin!

FATHER: Kerstin, yes! Have you taken a dip, my child?

SON: No, she's had only a cold shower! (*The bell rings.*)

MOTHER: There! We'll go in!

SON (*to the* FATHER): Take my wife's arm and I'll take Adele!

FATHER: No, thanks. You keep Kerstin for yourself!

[CURTAIN]

Debit and Credit

One Act

Characters

MR. AXEL, *a doctor of philosophy and a traveler in Africa*

MR. TURE, *his brother, a gardener*

TURE'S WIFE (ANNA)

MISS CECILIA

HER FIANCÉ

DR. LINDGREN, *formerly a teacher*

MISS MARI

THE CHAMBERLAIN

THE WAITER

An attractive hotel room {in the 1890s}. Doors to the right and left. Ture and his wife {examining the room}.

TURE: This isn't just a high-class room! But then the man who has it is high-class.

WIFE: Yes, I'll say! I haven't ever seen your brother, but I've certainly heard about him instead.

TURE: Talk away! My brother, the doctor, has traveled through Africa, and it isn't everybody who does—no matter how much he drank when he was young . . .

WIFE: Your brother, the doctor! Who is only a teacher as far as that goes . . .

TURE: Oh no, he's a Ph.D. . . .

WIFE: Well, that's a teacher, isn't it! So's my brother in the school at Åby.

TURE: Your brother's a very good man, but he's only a public school teacher, and that's not up to a Ph.D., without bragging.

WIFE: Whatever he wants to be and whatever you want to call him, he certainly has cost us a lot!

TURE: Yes, it's been costly, but he's given us a great deal of satisfaction, too!

WIFE: What a satisfaction! We've lost both house and home because of him!

TURE: That's true, but we still don't know if he has had good reasons for not taking care of the loan. Most likely it isn't easy to send money from darkest Africa.

WIFE: Even if he did, that won't straighten out the mess; but if he wants to do something for us, it's only his duty.

TURE: We'll see! We'll see! Anyhow: have you heard he has been decorated four times?

WIFE: What good do his orders do us? I imagine he has become even more stuck up. Oh no, I won't soon forget, the sheriff had to come to us with his papers—and bring in people to witness—and then—that auction when all the neighbors had to come in to root about in our belongings! Do you know, Ture, what really hurt me most?

TURE: Your black . . .

WIFE: Yes, having my sister-in-law buy my black silk dress for fifteen crowns! Fifteen crowns!

TURE: Just wait! Just wait! We can certainly get you a new silk dress . . .

WIFE (*crying*): Yes, but we can never get that one—that my sister-in-law bought.

TURE: Then we can get another one! Look at that fine hat! It must be a royal chamberlain Axel's talking to!

WIFE: What do I care about that?

TURE: Well, don't you think it's fun that a person who has the same name as you and I is so respected he's called on by someone close to the king? I remember you were delighted for fourteen days when your brother the teacher was invited to have dinner with the bishop.

WIFE: I don't remember that!

TURE: No, I imagine not!

WIFE: But I do remember March 14 when we had to leave our place because of your brother, after having been married for two years and with a child in my arms. And, when the steamboat came with all those people on board. When we were going to move—I'll never forget that for all the cocked hats in the world! Besides, what do you think a royal chamberlain cares about a gardener's family that has been ejected?

TURE: Look at this! What is it? Look at his decorations! Look at this!

(*He takes an order out of its case on the desk, puts it in his hand and strokes it gently.*)

WIFE: Junk like that!

TURE: Don't say anything bad about decorations. We never know where we'll come to. The head gardener at Stäringe became a director and a knight of the Order of Vasa the other day.

WIFE: What good does that do us?

TURE: Not that, true, but these (*points at the orders*) could surely help us get another job. But this waiting's getting pretty long, so we might as well sit down and make ourselves at home. Let me help you take off your coat! Come on!

WIFE (*after slight resistance*): Do you think we'll be welcome? I have a feeling we won't be here very long!

TURE: Oh yes! And I expect a good dinner here if I know Axel. If he only knew we were here . . . But let's see! (*He presses a bell; a* WAITER *enters*) [*To his wife*] What would you like? A sandwich! Perhaps? (*To the* WAITER) Bring us two open-faced sandwiches and beer. Just a minute! A shot for me—aquavit! [*To his* WIFE] We'll look after ourselves, you'll see! (AXEL *and the* CHAMBERLAIN *enter.*)

AXEL (*to the* CHAMBERLAIN): Five o'clock with tails and white tie then!

CHAMBERLAIN: And your orders!

AXEL: Is that really necessary?

CHAMBERLAIN: Absolutely necessary, if you don't want to be impolite, and you don't want to be that to anyone since you're a democrat! Good-bye, Doctor!

AXEL: Good-bye!

(*The* CHAMBERLAIN *bows slightly to* TURE *and his* WIFE *just as he goes, but they do not respond.*)

AXEL: Well! It's you, old boy! It's been a long time! And your wife! Welcome! Welcome!

TURE: Thank you, brother! And welcome back from your long trip!

AXEL: Yes, that *was* a trip—you've read about it in the papers, I suppose—

TURE: Yes, indeed, I've read everything! (*Pause*) I have greetings from Father!

AXEL: Well, is he still angry with me?

TURE: Oh, you know the old man and his ways! If *you* hadn't been along on that expedition, he would have considered it one of the seven wonders of the world. But since you were along, the whole thing's humbug.

AXEL: So he's the same as ever. Because I'm *his* son, whatever I do won't do. At least he's not conceited! Well! That's that then!—But how are things going for you?

TURE: Not very well! That old bank loan . . .

AXEL: Yes, that, of course! Well, how did it go?

TURE: Well, I had to pay it.

AXEL: That's damnable. But we'll take care of that at the earliest opportunity.

(*The* WAITER *enters with a breakfast tray.*)

AXEL: What's this?

TURE: Oh, I took the liberty of ordering sandwiches . . .

AXEL: That was sensible! But we should drink a glass of wine with my sister-in-law since I couldn't be at the wedding.

TURE: No, thanks, not for us! Not in the forenoon! Thank you!

AXEL (*signals to the* WAITER, *who leaves*): I should really have taken you out for dinner, but I have to go to one myself. Can you guess where?

TURE: You're surely not going to the palace, are you?

AXEL: Yes, I'm to have dinner with the prince himself!

TURE: Good heavens!—What do you say to that, Anna?

(*His wife turns and twists, annoyed, without being able to answer.*)

AXEL: Father will become a republican after this, when he hears His Majesty wants to associate with me.

TURE: Listen, Axel! Forgive me for raising a rather unpleasant subject, but it's one we have to talk about.

AXEL: I suppose it's that blessed loan!

AXEL: Yes, but it's not only that. Bluntly—for your sake we've had to sell everything at a sheriff's auction and are absolutely penniless.

AXEL: That's terrible! But why didn't you renew the loan?

TURE: How could I? Where was I going to get a new lender when you were gone?

AXEL: You could certainly have gone to my friends.

TURE: I did! Well, the result was what it is! Can you help us now?

AXEL: How could I help you now? When all my creditors are after me? How am I going to begin borrowing when they're just about to make a place for me? There isn't any worse recommendation than borrowing. Just wait a little, and it'll all straighten out.

TURE: Do you think we can wait without being absolutely ruined? This is just the time when gardening's starting; now's the time to dig and sow if you're going to get any results at the right time. Can't you get us a job?

AXEL: Where should I take a gardener's job?

TURE: From your friends!

AXEL: My friends don't have gardens! Don't stand in my way when I'm trying to save myself! When I'm saved, I'll save you.

TURE (*to his wife*): He doesn't want to help us, Anna!

AXEL: I can't—now! Is it reasonable to expect me who's looking for a job, to try to get one for someone else? What would people say? Well, something like this: look at that—we're not only getting him but his relatives, too. And then they won't take me.

TURE (*looks at his watch; then to his* WIFE): We have to go!

AXEL: What's your hurry?

TURE: We have to take the baby to the doctor!

AXEL: Good God, do you have a child, too?

WIFE: Yes, we do! And a sick one, who became sick when we had to move into the kitchen when they forced us to auction off everything.

AXEL: And this for my sake; all this will drive me crazy! For my sake! So I could become a famous man! What can I do for you? But would I have had it better if I had stayed at home? Worse, because I'd still have been a poverty-stricken school teacher who surely would have been of less use to you than I am now! Listen! Go to the doctor, but come back in a little while and I'll have thought of something for you.

TURE (*to his* WIFE): There you see! He wants to help us!

WIFE: He ought to be able to!

TURE: He can do what he wants to!

AXEL: Just don't rely on that, for the last way can turn out worse than the first! Good God, you have a sick child, too! And for my sake!

TURE: Oh, it's probably not as bad as it sounds!

WIFE: That's what you say who don't understand anything . . .

TURE: So long, Axel! (LINDGREN *appears in the doorway.*)

WIFE (*to* TURE): He didn't introduce us! to the chamberlain!

TURE: Nonsense, what's the difference? (*They leave.*)

(AXEL *is startled by* LINDGREN, *who is somewhat shabbily dressed; sleepy, unshaven, looking as if he has been drinking.*)

LINDGREN: Do you recognize me?

AXEL: Yes, I do now; but you have changed a lot!

LINDGREN: You think so, do you?

AXEL: Yes, I do, and I'm amazed three years could make that much difference . . .

LINDGREN: Three years can be a long time! Aren't you going to ask me to sit down?

AXEL: Yes, but I'm in a bit of a hurry!

LINDGREN: You always were in a hurry! (*Sits down.*) (*Pause*)

AXEL: Say something unpleasant now!

LINDGREN: That'll come, that'll come! (*Wipes his glasses.*) (*Pause*)

AXEL: How much do you need?

LINDGREN: Three hundred fifty!

AXEL: I don't have that much and can't get it either!

LINDGREN: Oh yes you can! Excuse my taking a drop! (*He pours a drink.*)

AXEL: Wouldn't you do me the favor of taking a glass of wine instead?

LINDGREN: No, why?

AXEL: Well, it looks bad to see you drinking aquavit like that!

LINDGREN: You have become particular!

AXEL: It will hurt my reputation, my credit!

LINDGREN: If you have credit, you can help me up after dragging me down!

AXEL: That's to say, you're dunning me!

LINDGREN: I'm simply reminding you I'm one of your victims!

AXEL: Then with the gratitude I owe you I'd like to remind you: that you helped me take my examinations at the university, when you happened to have money, that you printed my dissertation . . .

LINDGREN: That I taught you your scholarly approach which determined your scholarly career, that I who then was respectable influenced your careless nature favorably, that I made you, in a word; and that when I finally tried to get the grant for the expedition, you got in my way and took it!

AXEL: Got it! Because they considered me the man for the project, and not you!

LINDGREN: And that finished me! One is taken up, the other left behind!—Did you think that was treating me decently?

AXEL: It was what they call ungrateful, but the assignment was carried out, scholarship advanced, the honor of our country upheld, and new countries opened to the benefit of coming generations!

LINDGREN: Skål! You've practiced oratory! Do you know how unpleasant it is to be the one who's used and discarded?

AXEL: I imagine it would feel damnably uncomfortable, and I congratulate you for not being in my false position! Let's get back to reality! What can I do for you?

LINDGREN: What do you think?

AXEL: At the moment, nothing!

LINDGREN: The next thing you'll be gone! And I'll never get to see you again! (*Pours himself another drink.*)

AXEL: Do me the favor of not emptying the bottle so I'll be suspected by the servants!

LINDGREN: Hold it!

AXEL: Do you think it's pleasant for me to have to correct you like this? Do you?

LINDGREN: Listen: Will you get me a ticket for the banquet tonight?

AXEL: I'm sorry to say that I don't think they'll let you in!

LINDGREN: Because . . .

AXEL: You're drunk!

LINDGREN: Thanks a lot, old friend! Listen, will you let me see your botanic collections then?

AXEL: No, I'm going to study those for the academy!

LINDGREN: What about your ethnographic ones then?

AXEL: No, they're not mine!

LINDGREN: Will you . . . give me twenty-five crowns then?

AXEL: I can't give you more than ten, since I haven't more than twenty!

LINDGREN: Damnation!

AXEL: That's how it is for the envied person! Do you think there's anyone with whom I can share my joy? No one! The ones below hate the person who has come up, and the ones above fear the one who has come up!

LINDGREN: Yes, you are unfortunate!

AXEL: You know, after what I've lived through the last half hour, I'm inclined to change places with you. How calm and invulnerable not to have anything to lose; how interesting and sympathy-arousing to be the little man, the misunderstood, the one passed by. You simply extend your hand and get a few coins right away; you offer your arm, and you have friends to support you; and what a mighty party the millions like you make! Enviable soul—you don't know your own good luck!

LINDGREN: So you think I'm that far down and you're that far up. Listen, you haven't happened to read this paper? (*Holds up a paper.*)

AXEL: No, and I don't want to read it either!

LINDGREN: But you ought to for your own sake!

AXEL: No, I certainly won't, not even for your pleasure. You're saying: Come here so I can spit on you, and you're naive enough to insist I'm really to come! You know what: I've just had the strong conviction that if I met you in a dense bamboo forest, I'd shoot you down without hesitation.

LINDGREN: I believe you, you beast of prey!

AXEL: A person should never close the books with one's friends or people one has lived intimately with, because one never knows who has the most figures in debit! But when you come with your bill, I'll take a close look at it! Don't you think I quickly noticed that behind your helpfulness was an unconscious desire to convert me into the strong arm you lacked and which was to carry out what you couldn't? I had ideas and initiative, but you had only money and contacts. So I can congratulate myself you didn't eat me alive, and I can be excused for consuming you since the only choice I had was eat or be eaten!

LINDGREN: Beast!

AXEL: Rat, who couldn't rise to be a beast of prey! as you really wanted. Just as right now you don't wish you were up here with me, but to have me down with you. If you have anything important to add, hurry; I'm expecting company.

LINDGREN: Your fiancée?

AXEL: So you've already spied that out, too!

LINDGREN: Yes, indeed! And I know what Mari, whom you deserted, is thinking and saying; and I know what has happened to your brother and sister-in-law . . .

AXEL: So you know my girl friend! You see, I'm not engaged yet.

LINDGREN: No, but I know her boy friend!

AXEL: What do you mean?

LINDGREN: She has been going with someone else the whole time . . . So, you didn't know?

AXEL (*listening toward the exit door*): Yes, I did know, but I thought she had broken off with him! Listen, won't you come back in a quarter hour—I'll try to arrange something for you, somehow!

LINDGREN: Is this getting rid of me more nicely?

AXEL: No! It's an attempt at paying off a relationship! Seriously!

LINDGREN: Then I'll go, and come back . . . Until then . . .
  (*The* WAITER, *later the* BOY FRIEND *dressed in black and wearing the Temperance Society's ribbon enter.*)

WAITER: Doctor, a gentleman's here to see you!

AXEL: Have him come in!
  (*The* WAITER *goes, leaving the door open. The* BOY FRIEND *enters.*)

LINDGREN (*looks at* AXEL *searchingly*): Good-bye, Axel! Good luck! (*Goes.*)

AXEL: Good-bye! Whom do I have the honor . . .

BOY FRIEND (*embarrassed*): My name isn't a big name, like yours, Doctor, and my errand is a matter of the heart . . .

AXEL: Are *you* . . . You know Miss Cecilia?

BOY FRIEND: I'm the one!

AXEL (*at first hesitant, then more firmly*): Won't you sit down? (*Opens the door and signals to the* WAITER.)

AXEL (*to the* WAITER): Get my bill ready, pack my baggage in there, and have a taxi ready in half an hour.

WAITER (*bows and leaves*): Yes, Doctor!

AXEL (*up to the* BOY FRIEND; *sits down on a chair*): Please say what you have to say!

BOY FRIEND (*after a pause, unctuously*): Two men were in the same city, the one rich, the other poor. The rich man had sheep and cattle in abundance; the poor man owned nothing except a little lamb . . .

AXEL: Is that any of my business?

BOY FRIEND (*as before*): . . . a little lamb, which he had bought and which he raised . . .

AXEL: Come to the point! What do you want? Are you still engaged to Miss Cecilia?

BOY FRIEND (*changing his manner*): Have I said anything about any Cecilia? Have I?

AXEL: Tell me what you came to say, or I'll show you out! But

do it quickly and correctly, without beating about the bush
. . .

BOY FRIEND (*offering* AXEL *snuff*): Would you have some?

AXEL: No, thanks!

BOY FRIEND: A big shot doesn't have small weaknesses like that.

AXEL: Well, since you don't want to talk, I will. It's really not your business, but it might do you good to know it since you don't seem to; I am going to exchange rings with Miss Cecilia, who was engaged to you.

BOY FRIEND (*hit*): Was?

AXEL: Yes, she has broken her engagement to you, hasn't she?

BOY FRIEND: Not that I know!

AXEL (*takes a ring from his vest pocket*): Strange, that you didn't know. You do now! Take a look at my ring!

BOY FRIEND: She has broken off her engagement to me?

AXEL: Since she can't be engaged to two at the same time and since she doesn't like you any more, she had to break her engagement to you! I'd have told you all this much more gently if you hadn't offended me when you came in!

BOY FRIEND: I haven't offended you!

AXEL: Cowardly and false, fawning and showoffish!

BOY FRIEND (*gently*): You are a hard man, Doctor!

AXEL: No, but I'm becoming one! You haven't spared my feelings; you sneered, but I didn't. This conference is over.

BOY FRIEND (*genuinely moved*): It was my only lamb, which I was afraid you'd take away from me, but you don't want to do that, you who have so many . . .

AXEL: Assume I really didn't want to—would you be sure she'd want to be loyal to you?

BOY FRIEND: Think of me, Doctor!

AXEL: Yes, if you think of me!

BOY FRIEND: I'm a poor man . . .

Jarl Kulle and Doris Hedlund in *Playing with Fire*, Royal
Dramatic Theater, 1957.

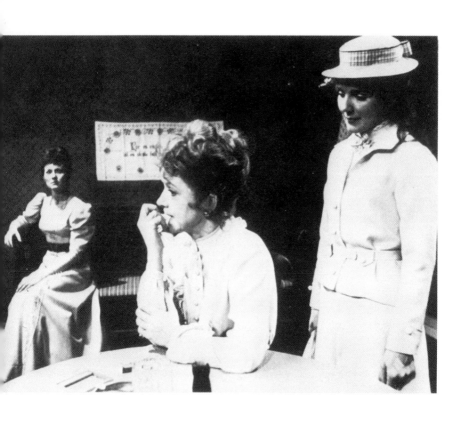

Agneta Prytz, Nadja Witzansky, and Nini Witzansky in *Mother Love*, TV, 1967.

Lars Hanson and Anders Henrikson in *Pariah*, Royal
Dramatic Theater, 1949.

Rosa-Berit Gelin and Carl Hugo Callander in *The First Warning*, TV, 1967.

AXEL: So am I! But you have, from what I can see and hear, an expectation of eternal bliss beyond this life! I don't! As far as that goes, I haven't taken anything from you—I've only taken what has been offered to me! Just as you have!

BOY FRIEND: And I who have dreamt of a future for this girl, a future so bright . . .

AXEL: Excuse my saying something impolite to you, since you're being impolite to me: Are you so sure this girl's future can't be still brighter at my side . . .

BOY FRIEND: You're reminding me of my humble position as a laborer . . .

AXEL: No, I'm reminding you of this girl's future, which is so close to your heart, and when I hear she no longer loves you but loves me, I take the liberty of thinking her future brighter with the one she loves than with the one she doesn't love!

BOY FRIEND: You are strong, and we little people are made to be sacrificed!

AXEL: Listen, I've been told that you forced a rival for Cecilia's hand out of the way, and not with too honorable means. What do you think that victim thought of you?

BOY FRIEND: He was a bad man!

AXEL: From whom you saved the girl! Now I'm saving her from you! Good-bye! (CECILIA *enters*.)

BOY FRIEND: Cecilia! (CECILIA *flinches*.) You already know the way over here!

AXEL (*to the* BOY FRIEND): GET OUT OF HERE!

CECILIA: Give me a glass of water!

BOY FRIEND (*picks up the aquavit bottle*): The carafe seems to have been emptied! Watch out for that man, Cecilia!

AXEL (*pushing the* BOY FRIEND *out*): Your presence is absolutely superfluous—get out!

BOY FRIEND: Watch out for that man, Cecilia! (*Leaves*.)

AXEL: This was a most unpleasant scene, and you could have

spared me by breaking openly with him and by not coming to my room!

CECILIA (*bursts into tears*): Am I to be scolded on top of everything!

AXEL: The blame had to be fixed, and now when that's settled—we'll talk about something else! To start with: How do you feel?

CECILIA: So—so!

AXEL: Then you're not feeling well?

CECILIA: How do you feel yourself?

AXEL: Fine, but I'm a little tired!

CECILIA: Will you go with me to my aunt's this afternoon?

AXEL: No, I can't, for I'm going out to dinner.

CECILIA: And that's more fun! You go out so often, I never get to!

AXEL: Hm!

CECILIA: What do you mean—hm?

AXEL: Your comment made an unpleasant impression on me!

CECILIA: A person gets so many unpleasant impressions these days . . .

AXEL: For example?

CECILIA: When one reads the papers!

AXEL: You've read the scandals about me! Do you believe them?

CECILIA: What am I to believe?

AXEL: So you suspect I'm the dishonorable person they say I am in those stories, and since you still want to marry me, I have to assume you'll do that out of practical motives and not because of personal feelings.

CECILIA: You're speaking so harshly, as if you didn't like me at all!

AXEL: Cecilia! Will you leave with me in a quarter of an hour?

CECILIA: In a quarter hour? Where would we go?

AXEL: To London!

CECILIA: I won't go with you until we're married!

AXEL: Why?

CECILIA: Why do we have to go away in such a hurry?

AXEL: Because—it's suffocating here! If we stay, I'll be pulled down so far I'll never come up again!

CECILIA: That's strange! Are things that bad?

AXEL: Will you come with me or won't you?

CECILIA: Not before we're married because you won't marry me afterwards!

AXEL: So that's your belief! Sit down then for a moment while I go in there to write a couple letters!

CECILIA: Am I to sit here alone with the doors open?

AXEL: Don't close the door; then we're absolutely lost. (*Going out to the left.*)

CECILIA: But don't stay too long! (*She goes up to the exit door and turns the key. {A moment later} MARI comes in through that door.*)

CECILIA: Wasn't the door closed?

MARI: Not so I could notice! Well, so it was to be shut?

CECILIA: Whom do I have the honor?

MARI: With whom do I?

CECILIA: That's none of your business!

MARI: Nice! Now I understand! So, it's you! Then I'm your victim—for the time being!

CECILIA: I don't know you!

MARI: But I know you all the better!

CECILIA (*gets up, goes to the left door*): So-o! (*In the doorway to* AXEL) Come out here for a minute!

[AXEL *appears*]

AXEL (*to* MARI): What do you want?

MARI: One never knows!

AXEL: Get out then!

MARI: Why?

AXEL: Because what there was between us was over three years ago!

MARI: And now there's someone else, who's to be thrown on the garbage dump!

AXEL: Did I ever promise you anything I didn't keep? Do I owe you anything? Did I ever mention marriage? Did we have children together? Have I been the only one to enjoy your favors?

MARI: But now you're thinking of being the only one? With that creature?

CECILIA (*goes up to* MARI): Keep still! I don't know you!

MARI: When we were on the streets we knew each other; and when we were on the prowl I remember we called each other by our first names! (*To* AXEL) And now you're going to marry that thing! You know you're absolutely too good for that!

AXEL (*to* CECILIA): Do you know this girl?

CECILIA: No!

MARI: Aren't you ashamed! I didn't know you at first, because you're so nicely dressed . . .

    (AXEL *fixes* CECILIA's *glance.*)

CECILIA: Come! I'll go with you!

AXEL (*preoccupied with his thoughts*): Right away! Just wait a little! I'll go in to write one more letter! But now we'll shut the door first!

MARI: No thanks, I don't want to be shut up as she was when I came!

AXEL (*startled to extreme attention*): Was the door shut?

CECILIA (*to* MARI): Can you insist the door was shut?

MARI: Since you thought it was, I assumed you had shut it so carelessly it opened . . .

AXEL (*looks questioningly at* CECILIA; *then to* MARI): Mari, you

were a kind girl it seemed to me. Will you return my
letters now?

MARI: No!

AXEL: What are you going to do with them?

MARI: I can sell them, I've heard, now that you've become
such a famous man.

AXEL: And you can get revenge through them!

MARI: Yes!

AXEL: Is it Lindgren . . . ?

MARI: Yes! . . . There he is himself! (LINDGREN *enters, now
in a good mood.*)

LINDGREN: Well, look at the girls! And Mari's here, too—as
the joker in every game! Listen, Axel!

AXEL: I hear you even when I don't see you! You're in a good
mood! What has gone wrong for me now?

LINDGREN: I was a bit down this morning before I could pull
myself together, but then I had a good beefsteak . . .
Well! You see! You don't really owe me anything [AXEL
looks amazed] for what I've done, I've done out of the
goodness of my heart, and I've had both honor and
pleasure from that, and what you've got, you've been given
and haven't borrowed!

AXEL: You're entirely too modest and generous!

LINDGREN: Don't say that! Still a favor in return: Will you
sign this note for me? (AXEL *hesitant.*) Don't be afraid; I'm
not going to embarrass you as your brother . . .

AXEL: What do you mean? Why, I'm the one who has ruined
him . . .

LINDGREN: For two hundred, yes, but you underwrote his
five-year lease . . .

AXEL: Good God!

LINDGREN: What's that?—Hm, hm!

AXEL (*looks at his watch*): Wait a couple minutes; I'll go in to
write a couple letters! (CECILIA *wants to go with him but he*

keeps her back.) A couple minutes, my dear . . . (*Kisses her on her forehead.*) A couple minutes! (*Going to the left.*)

LINDGREN: Here's the document! Sign it right away!

AXEL: Give it to me! (*Takes it and goes out determinedly to the left.*)

LINDGREN: Well, you're on good terms now, girls?

MARI: Oh yes! And before we leave together we'll be on still better terms! (CECILIA *looks scornful.*) I think I'd like to have some fun today!

LINDGREN: Come out with me; I'll get money!

MARI: No!

(CECILIA *uneasy, sits down by the door through which* AXEL *has gone, as if seeking support.*)

LINDGREN: We'll go look at the fireworks tonight; then we can see how a great man looks in illumination. Right, Cissy?

CECILIA: You know, I'll be sick if I stay here.

MARI: That wouldn't be the first time!

LINDGREN: Go to it, girls, so I can hear it! Quarrel so it hails about the ears—eh! (TURE *and his* WIFE *enter.*) Look! Old acquaintances! How are you?

TURE: Fine, thank you!

LINDGREN: And the baby?

TURE: The baby?

LINDGREN: So you've already forgotten the baby? Do you have as hard a time remembering names?

TURE: Names?

LINDGREN: Signatures? Terrible how slowly he's writing in there!

TURE: Is my brother, the doctor, in there?

LINDGREN: If the doctor's in there I don't know, but your brother went in there a while ago! We might as well find out. (*Knocks on the door.*) Silent as the grave! (*Knocks again.*) Then I'll go in! (*Goes in. Everyone uneasy and tense.*)

CECILIA: What does this mean?

MARI: We'll see!

TURE: What has gone on here?

WIFE: There's something going on . . . you'll see he won't help us!

LINDGREN (*comes out of the room with a bottle and some letters*): What does it say on this? (*Reads on the bottle.*) Cyanide! Imagine, how stupid he was, that sensitive fool, to commit suicide because of that little. (*General crying out.*) So you weren't a beast of prey, my dear Axel! But . . . (*Looks back into the room.*) He isn't there . . . neither are his things. So he's gone! And the bottle's unopened—that means: he intended to take his life but changed his mind! Look, here we have the messages he left. "To Miss Cecilia. . ." seems to contain something round—probably an engagement ring . . . There you are! "To my brother Ture . . . (*Holds the letter up to the light.*) With a blue paper . . . it's a draft for . . . the amount! You're welcome! (*The* BOY FRIEND *shows up in the door to the right.*)

TURE (*who has opened his letter*): Look, he helped us all the same . . .

WIFE: Yes, in that way!

LINDGREN: And here's my promissory note!—without his signature! That's a strong man! Damnation!

MARI: So the fireworks are canceled!

BOY FRIEND: Wasn't there anything for me?

LINDGREN: Yes, there's a fiancée, I think, over there! Imagine, what a man, all the same, to be able to straighten out his shaky finances! It does annoy me, of course, that I let myself be fooled, but, the devil take me I think I would have done the same thing . . . Maybe you, too? Eh?

[CURTAIN]

Mother Love

One Act

Characters

THE MOTHER, *formerly a prostitute, forty-two years old*
THE DAUGHTER (*Hélène*), *an actress, twenty years old*
LISEN, *eighteen years old*
A DRESSER *at the theater*

The interior of a fisherman's cottage at a bathing resort. The background is a glass-enclosed veranda facing a channel in the archipelago.

The MOTHER *and the* DRESSER *are smoking cigars, drinking porter and playing cards. The* DAUGHTER *at the window looking out, intensely watchful.*

MOTHER: Come on, Hélène, take a hand!

DAUGHTER: Can't I get out of playing cards on such a beautiful summer day?

DRESSER: Always be kind to your mother!

MOTHER: Don't sit on the porch right in the sun getting sunburned!

DAUGHTER: It doesn't burn here!

MOTHER: Then there's a draft! (*to the* DRESSER) Your deal! Go ahead!

DAUGHTER: Mayn't I go bathing with the girls today?

MOTHER: Not without your mother—you know that!

DAUGHTER: Yes, but the girls can swim, and you can't!

MOTHER: It's not a question of who can swim and who can't, but you know, Hélène, you're never to go anywhere without your mother.

DAUGHTER: Don't I know! I've heard that ever since I could understand what you were saying.

DRESSER: That shows you've had a loving mother who has wanted what's best for you . . . Yes, it does!

MOTHER (*takes the* DRESSER's *hand*): Thank you! Thank you

for those words, Augusta! How I've otherwise been that
. . . but I've been a loving mother—I can safely say that
myself.

DAUGHTER: Well, then I suppose there's no point in asking if
I can play tennis either!

DRESSER: You shouldn't be impudent to your mother, young
lady, and when you don't want to please those closest to
you by sharing their simple pleasures, to say the least it
hurts when you ask to have a good time with other people!

DAUGHTER: Yes, yes, I know all that; I know, I know!

MOTHER: Are you being naughty again? Do something
useful, don't sit there doing nothing! You're grownup!

DAUGHTER: If I'm grownup, why do you treat me like a
child?

MOTHER: Because you behave like one!

DAUGHTER: You shouldn't scold me for that since you want
to keep me like one!

MOTHER: Listen, Hélène, you seem to have started quibbling
lately . . . Whom are you associating with here?

DAUGHTER: With you two, among others!

MOTHER: So you're starting to keep secrets from your
mother?

DAUGHTER: Yes, it's about time!

DRESSER: Shame on you, you brat! Are you going to talk back
to your mother?

MOTHER: We should do something useful instead of
bickering. Read your part to me, for example!

DAUGHTER: The director told me not to read it to others
since they teach me what's wrong . . .

MOTHER: Well-l, that's the thanks I get for wanting to help!
And I suppose everything I do is stupid!

DAUGHTER: Why do you do it then? And why should I be
blamed when you do something crazy!

DRESSER: So you want to remind your mother she's not educated! Shame on you, that's low!

DAUGHTER: You say I want to, but I don't. But when Mother wants to teach me what's wrong, I have to speak up, if I'm not to lose my contract and we're to have an income!

MOTHER: So now you're telling us you support us. But do you know what you owe Aunt Augusta? Do you know it was she who took care of us both when your good-for-nothing father deserted us, that she supported us, so that you can never pay her for what you owe her? Do you know that? (*The* DAUGHTER *remains silent.*) Do you? Answer me!

DAUGHTER: I won't answer that!

MOTHER: You won't answer!

DRESSER: Take it easy, Amalie! The neighbors can hear us, and then there'll be talk! There, calm yourself!

MOTHER (*to the* DAUGHTER): Put on your coat, and we'll go for a walk!

DAUGHTER: I don't want to take a walk today!

MOTHER: That's the third day you've refused to go walking with your mother! (*Speculating.*) Is it possible? Go out on the veranda, Hélène, while I talk with your Aunt Augusta.

(*The* DAUGHTER *goes out on the veranda.*)

MOTHER: Do you think it's possible?

DRESSER: What?

MOTHER: That she has heard something?

DRESSER: That's impossible!

MOTHER: Anything can happen! Not that I believe anyone can have been so cruel as to tell the child directly. I had a nephew who was thirty-six years old before he found out his father was a suicide . . . But there *is* something back of Hélène's change in behavior. Eight days ago I noticed she was uncomfortable having me along on the promenade. She wanted to take only out-of-the-way paths; when we met anyone, she looked away; she was nervous, I couldn't get a word out of her and she wanted to go home! There *is* something!

DRESSER: Could she have been—if I've understood you—been embarrassed by your company—her own mother's company?

MOTHER: Yes!

DRESSER: Well, that's going too far!

MOTHER: Yes, and what's worse: Can you imagine, she didn't introduce me when we came out on the steamboat and friends of hers came up to us?

DRESSER: Do you know what I think? She has met someone who has arrived the last eight days. We'll go down to the post office to find out who has arrived lately.

MOTHER: Yes, that's what we'll do! (*calls out*) Hélène! Look after the house for a while while we go to the post office!

DAUGHTER (*comes in*): Yes, Mother!

MOTHER (*to the* DRESSER): It's absolutely as if I had dreamt this already . . .

DRESSER: Yes, one's dreams come back sometimes . . . I know that—but not the pleasant ones! (*They go out to the right.*)

(*The* DAUGHTER *signals.* LISEN *enters dressed for tennis, a white costume with a white hat.*)

LISEN: Have they left?

DAUGHTER: Yes, for a while.

LISEN: Well, what did your mother say?

DAUGHTER: I didn't dare ask her! She gets upset so easily!

LISEN: Poor Hélène! So you won't come along on the picnic! And I'd been so happy about that . . . If you only knew how much I like you! (*Kisses her.*)

DAUGHTER: If you only knew how much knowing you and being in your home these days have meant to me—I've never been out among people with good manners before.

Imagine how I've felt—I've lived in a stuffy little town among people with an uncertain, mysterious existence, whispering, squabbling, complaining, people who have never said a friendly word to me, still less shown they like me, and have kept watch over me as if I were a prisoner to be punished . . . It's my mother I'm talking about, and that hurts me, very, very much!

LISEN: One can't be blamed for what kind of parents one has, and . . .

DAUGHTER: No, but one has to suffer for it! They say one can live out one's life without finding out what kind of people one's parents are even though one has lived with them. And I suppose so, for if one did find out, one wouldn't believe it!

LISEN (*embarrassed*): Have you heard anything?

DAUGHTER: Yes, when I was at the baths three days ago, I heard some people on the other side of the partition talking about my mother. Do you know what they said?

LISEN: Don't bother about that . . .

DAUGHTER: They said she had been a bad woman!—I didn't want to believe it; I still don't, but I feel it's true; everything fits together to make it likely—and I'm ashamed! I'm ashamed to be seen with her, I feel people are looking at us; that the men are staring . . . why, it's terrible! But is it true? Do you think it's true?

LISEN: People lie so much, and I don't know!

DAUGHTER: Yes, you do, you do know something, but you don't want to tell me, and I thank you for that, but I'm just as unhappy either way, whether you tell me or not!

LISEN: Forget about this and come over to our place and you'll meet people you'll like. My father came home this morning and wants to see you—I've been telling him about you in my letters to him, and I think my cousin Gerhard has, too.

DAUGHTER: You do have a father; I did, too, when I was very, very young . . .

LISEN: Where did he go?

DAUGHTER: He deserted us, because he was a bad man, Mother says!

LISEN: It's hard to know about that . . . Still—I'll tell you one more thing: If you come home with me today, you'll meet the director of the leading theater, and there's a chance you'll land a contract.

DAUGHTER: What are you saying?

LISEN: Well, that's how it is, and he's interested in you, and you know how a little thing can change lives: a personal meeting, a good word put in at the right time. You can't say "no" without standing in your own way.

DAUGHTER: I do want to! But you see I don't go anywhere without Mother.

LISEN: Why? Can you give me one reason?

DAUGHTER: I don't know! She taught me to say that as a child, and I haven't got over it.

LISEN: Did she make you promise?

DAUGHTER: No, she didn't need to; she simply said: Say that! So I've been saying it!

LISEN: Do you think you'd be unfair to her if you were away from her for a few hours?

DAUGHTER: I don't think she'd miss me, for when I'm at home she always has something to criticize about me; but I'd feel guilty that I went where she couldn't be along.

LISEN: Have you ever thought of bringing her along to my home?

DAUGHTER: No, good heavens, I've never thought of that!

LISEN: But when you get married . . .

DAUGHTER: I'm never going to get married!

LISEN: Has your mother taught you to say that, too?

DAUGHTER: Probably! Well, she has always warned me about men!

LISEN: Married men, too?

DAUGHTER: I suppose so!

LISEN: Listen, Hélène! You really need to free yourself!

DAUGHTER: Ugh! I certainly don't want to become a liberated woman!

LISEN: No, I don't mean one of those, but you need to free yourself from a dependency which you've outgrown and which could make life impossible for you.

DAUGHTER: I don't think I ever can. Imagine: my being forged to this mother from childhood on, never daring to think one thought that wasn't hers, never wishing for anything but what she wished! I know it holds me back, blocks me, but I can't do anything about it.

LISEN: And when your mother passes away, you'll be lost.

DAUGHTER: I'll have to put up with that.

LISEN: But you don't have any companions, not a friend; and a human being can't live isolated and alone. You have to try to get support! Haven't you ever been in love?

DAUGHTER: I don't know! I've never dared to think about anything like that, and Mother has never let any young man get interested in me! Would you fall in love?

LISEN: Yes, if someone liked me, and I wanted him!

DAUGHTER: Then you'll probably marry your cousin Gerhard!

LISEN: I never can—he doesn't care for me!

DAUGHTER: No?

LISEN: No! Since he cares for you!

DAUGHTER: Me?

LISEN: Yes, and one of my reasons for coming over was to deliver his request to call on you.

DAUGHTER: Here? No, that'll never do! And do you think I'd

want to stand in your way? Do you imagine I could replace you with him, you who are so beautiful, so nice . . . (*takes* LISEN's *hand.*) What a lovely hand! and wrist! I looked at your foot, dear, when we were in the baths last. (*Kneels before* LISEN *who has sat down.*) What a lovely foot. Every nail is perfect, the toes round and rosy red as a child's hand. (*Kisses* LISEN's *foot.*) You are a noblewoman made of other material than I.

LISEN: Stop that, and don't say crazy things! (*Gets up.*) If you knew! But . . .

DAUGHTER: And you must be just as good as you are beautiful. That's what those of us below always imagine when we look up at you with your light, soft features, where poverty hasn't traced its furrows, and envy hasn't torn its ugly lines.

LISEN: Listen, Hélène, I might think you have a crush on me . . .

DAUGHTER: Well, I do! I may resemble you a little, as a hepatica resembles an anemone; that's why I see my better self in you, something I'd like to be but never can. Light and white as an angel you came my way those last summer days; now it's fall, and the day after tomorrow we're moving back into town . . . We'll never know each other any more . . . And we shouldn't . . . You can never raise me, but I can pull you down, and I don't want to! I want you way, way up, and so far away I can't see your flaws. So: Good-bye, Lisen—my first and only friend . . .

LISEN: That's enough! Hélène! Do you know who I am? Well, I'm your sister!

DAUGHTER: You? What do you mean?

LISEN: You and I have the same father!

DAUGHTER: You're my sister, my little sister. But what does my father do? I suppose he's a commander since your

father is. How stupid I am! But he's married, since . . . Is
he good to you? He wasn't to my mother . . .

LISEN: You don't know that! But aren't you glad you've
received a little sister—that's to say one who doesn't cry?

DAUGHTER: Oh yes, I'm so glad I don't know what to say . . .
(*They embrace each other.*) But I don't dare to be really glad,
because I don't know what's going to happen now! What
will Mother say? And how will it be when we meet Father?

LISEN: Let me handle your mother; she'll soon be here—just
stay in the background until you're needed! So give me a
kiss first, dear. (*They kiss.*)

DAUGHTER: My sister! How strange that word sounds; so
does the word Father, when one hasn't said it . . .

LISEN: Let's not talk nonsense now but stick to the subject
. . . Do you think your mother will say no if you are
invited to our home? To your sister's and father's home?

DAUGHTER: Without Mother? Oh, she hates your—my father
terribly.

LISEN: But if she hasn't any cause? If you only knew how full
of lies and imaginings the world is! And of mistakes, and
misunderstandings! My father told about a friend of his
who went to sea as a cadet. A gold watch was stolen from
an officer's cabin, and the cadet was suspected. God knows
why. His comrades avoided him, and that made him bitter
so he became impossible, got into fights, and had to resign.
Two years later the thief was discovered—he was a sailor,
but they couldn't set things right for the innocent man
because he had only been suspected. The suspicion lasted
all through life even though he had been freed of blame;
and a nickname he had been given he had to keep. It had
grown like a house, been built and piled up on his false
reputation, so that when they were going to tear down the
false foundation the building was still there, hovering in

the air like the palace in *A Thousand and One Nights*. You see that's how it can go in this world! But it can go in a still crazier way as it did for the instrument maker in Arboga, who got the name Incendiary, Arsonist because someone had set a fire at his place, or like a certain Andersson who was called Thief Anders, because he had been the victim of a widely known theft.

DAUGHTER: You mean my father isn't what I think he is?

LISEN: Exactly!

DAUGHTER: I've seen him like this in my dreams sometimes since I've forgotten my memories of him. Isn't he rather tall, with a dark beard and big blue sailor's eyes?

LISEN: Yes, approximately!

DAUGHTER: And then . . . Wait, now I remember . . . Look at this watch! There's a little compass on the chain—and in the compass there's an eye where it says north! Who gave it to me?

LISEN: Your father! I was along when he bought it!

DAUGHTER: Then it's he I've seen at the theater so many times when I've been acting . . . He has always sat in a box to the left keeping his opera glasses on me—I never dared tell Mother, because she was always so protective. And once he brought me flowers, but Mother burned them up. Do you think it was he?

LISEN: It was he, and you may depend on it his eye has been kept on you all these years just as the eye has followed the needle on the compass.

DAUGHTER: And you say I'll get to see him, that he wants to see me! It's like a fairytale . . .

LISEN: No more fairytales! I hear your mother coming . . . Step out so I can take her on first!

DAUGHTER: It'll be dreadful, I can feel it! Why shouldn't people be able to get along and keep the peace! If it were only over! If Mother wanted to be kind . . . I'll pray to

God out there He'll make her kind . . . But He can't I
suppose, or doesn't want to, I don't know why!

LISEN: He can and wants to if you simply could believe in
happiness a little, and in your own ability . . .

DAUGHTER: Ability? For what? To be ruthless? I can't! And
enjoying happiness bought with other people's tears can't
last.

LISEN: There! Step back!

DAUGHTER: Imagine: you can believe this will end well!

LISEN: Sh-h! (HÉLÈNE *steps back, her* MOTHER *enters.*) Mrs. . . . .

MOTHER (*quickly*): Miss, if you please . . .

LISEN: Your daughter . . .

MOTHER: Yes, I have a daughter, though I'm not married, and
I suppose many women do, and I'm not ashamed of that
. . . What's this about?

LISEN: I really came over to ask if Miss Hélène could come
along on a picnic some of us have arranged.

MOTHER: Hasn't Hélène answered that herself?

LISEN: Yes, she answered I should ask you!

MOTHER: That wasn't a frank answer—Hélène, my child! Do
you want to go if your mother isn't along?

DAUGHTER: Yes, if you let me!

MOTHER: I let you? What have I to say about such a big girl?
Tell this girl how you want it: if you want your mother to
sit at home alone with her shame while you're out having a
good time; if you want to have people ask for your mother
and you have to avoid answering: "She wasn't invited"; and
because and because. Say how you want it yourself.

LISEN (*to the* MOTHER): Let's not twist words. I know fully
what Hélène wants and I understand your way of getting
her to answer the way you want her to. If you really love
your daughter as you insist, you'd want what's best for her
even if it were humiliating for yourself.

MOTHER: Listen, child. I know your name and who you are

though I haven't had the honor of being presented, but I wonder if your youth has anything to teach my age.

LISEN: Who knows? For six years since my mother died, I've spent my time bringing up my younger brothers and sisters, and I know there are people who never learn anything from life, no matter how old they get.

MOTHER: What are you trying to say?

LISEN: Something like this: now there's a chance for your daughter to get out into life, probably either to get her talent acknowledged or get engaged to a young man of good standing . . .

MOTHER: That sounds fine, but what are you going to do with me?

LISEN: It isn't a question of you, but of your daughter! Can't you think of her for a second without thinking about yourself?

MOTHER: Yes, you see when I'm thinking about myself, I'm thinking about my daughter, too, for she has learned to love her mother . . .

LISEN: I don't believe it! She has clung to you because you kept her away from everybody else, and she had to cling to someone when you tore her from her father.

MOTHER: What are you saying?

LISEN: That you tore her from her father when he refused to marry you when you had been unfaithful to him. You kept him from seeing his child, and you avenged your crime on him and on your child!

MOTHER: Hélène! Don't believe a word she says! To think that I have to live through a stranger's coming into my rooms to insult me in my own child's presence!

DAUGHTER (*comes forward*): You may not say anything bad about my mother . . .

LISEN: I can't help it when I'm saying something good about my father . . . Still I can hear this talk is almost over . . .

So let me give you a bit of advice or two. Get rid of that procuress you call Aunt Augusta if you don't want to have your daughter's reputation totally destroyed. That's number one! Then keep track of all the receipts for the money you've received from my father for Hélène's education, for you'll have to account for it soon! That was number two! And here's something extra! Quit forcing yourself on your daughter when she's out walking, and above all at the theater, or every chance of getting parts will be closed to her; and after that you'll sell her favors, just as you have tried to buy back your lost reputation at the cost of her future. (*The* MOTHER *is collapsing.*)

DAUGHTER (*to* LISEN): Leave this house. You who don't hold anything sacred, not even motherhood.

LISEN: Sacred! Just as when boys spit and say *pax*, then they're sacred, too.

DAUGHTER: It seems to me now as if you came over only to destroy and not at all to restore . . .

LISEN: Yes, I came to restore—my father, who was innocent, just as the arsonist against whom someone committed arson. I came to restore you, you, who were the victim of a woman, who can be raised up only by withdrawing to a place where no one will disturb her and where she'll not disturb others. That's why I came. Now I'm through! Good-bye!

MOTHER: Don't go until I've said a word! You came, too—disregarding that other nonsense—to invite Hélène to your home.

LISEN: Yes, and to give her a chance to meet the director of the leading theater who's interested in her.

MOTHER: What's that? The director! And you don't tell me that! Well! Hélène may go, alone! Yes, without me! (*The* DAUGHTER *gestures.*)

LISEN: Well, so you're human all the same! Hélène, you may come! Did you hear that!

DAUGHTER: Yes, but now I don't want to!

MOTHER: What are you saying!

DAUGHTER: No! I'll not fit in, I won't be comfortable among those who despise my mother!

MOTHER: But that's silly! Are you going to stand in your own way? Go ahead, get dressed, so you're all set!

DAUGHTER: No, I can't, I can't leave you, Mother, now that I know everything. I'll never have a happy moment again . . . I'll never be able to believe anything any more . . .

LISEN (*to the* MOTHER): There you reap what you've sowed—and if a man comes one fine day to take your daughter home, you'll sit there alone in your old age and have time to repent your lack of wisdom. Good-bye! (*Goes up to Hélène and kisses her on her forehead.*) Good-bye, sister dear!

DAUGHTER: Good-bye!

LISEN: Look me in the eyes as if you had some hope in living!

DAUGHTER: I can't! I can't thank you for your good will, for you have hurt me more than you know. You woke me up with a serpent, when I had fallen asleep on a hillside in the sunshine . . .

LISEN: Go to sleep again, and I'll wake you up with flowers and song! Good-night! And sleep well! (*Goes. The* DRESSER *enters.*)

MOTHER: An angel of light in white clothing! Well, it was a devil! A real devil! And you! How stupid you were! What nonsense! To be so sensitive when people are so crude!

DAUGHTER: To think you've lied to me so I've been fooled into lying about my father for so many years . . .

MOTHER: Oh, what's the use of talking about what's past . . .

DAUGHTER: And—Aunt Augusta!

MOTHER: Quiet, Aunt Augusta is a splendid woman to whom you owe a lot . . .

DAUGHTER: But that wasn't true either . . . Why, it was my father who paid for my education.

MOTHER: Yes, but I had to live, too . . . you're so small-minded. And vengeful, too! Can't you forget a little fib like that . . . There, there's Augusta! Come along, and we little people will amuse ourselves as well as we can.

DRESSER: Well, so it was he all the same! I didn't guess so badly, did I?

MOTHER: Well, we won't bother about that scoundrel . . .

DAUGHTER: Don't say that when it isn't true!

DRESSER: What is it that isn't true?

DAUGHTER: Come on, let's play cards! I can't tear down the walls you've needed so many years to build! Come on! (*She sits down at the card table and begins to meld the cards.*)

MOTHER: Well, finally—you're a sensible girl!

[CURTAIN]

The First Warning

A Comedy in One Act

Characters

THE HUSBAND *(Axel Brunner), 37*
THE WIFE *(Olga Brunner), 36*
ROSA, *15*
THE BARONESS, *Rosa's widowed mother, 47*

Setting

In Germany in the 1890s

A German dining room: a long dining table in the middle of the room; a large cupboard to the right; a tile stove, etc.

The door at the back is open so that one can see hills covered with vineyards, a steeple, etc.

A wallpapered door to the left. An overnight bag on a chair next to the cupboard. The WIFE *is writing at the table, on which are a bouquet of flowers and a pair of gloves. The* HUSBAND *enters.*

HUSBAND: Good morning, though it's noon. Did you sleep well?

WIFE: Splendidly, in view of circumstances!

HUSBAND: Well, we could have left the party a little earlier last night . . .

WIFE: It seems to me you said that last night a great many times . . .

HUSBAND (*picks up the bouquet*): Imagine, you remember that?

WIFE: I remember, too, that you didn't like my singing so many songs . . . Quit ruining my flowers!

HUSBAND: Were they the captain's?

WIFE: Yes, and most likely the gardener's before they became the florist's. But now they're mine.

HUSBAND (*tosses the bouquet down*): It's a lovely custom hereabouts to send flowers to other men's wives!

WIFE: You should have gone home to bed earlier, I think.

HUSBAND: I'm absolutely sure the captain would have liked

that. But since I could only choose between staying and being ridiculous or going home alone and being ridiculous, I stayed . . .

WIFE: And were comical!

HUSBAND: Can you explain how you want to be a comical husband's wife? I wouldn't want to be the husband of a ridiculous wife!

WIFE: It's too bad about you!

HUSBAND: Don't you think so? I do, quite often. But do you know what's tragic about my being ridiculous?

WIFE: Answer that yourself; then it'll be wittier than if I say it!

HUSBAND: . . . in my being in love with my wife after fifteen years of marriage . . .

WIFE: Fifteen years! Do you wear a pedometer?

HUSBAND (*sits down beside his* WIFE): On my thorny path? No! But you who dance along on a path strewn with roses probably ought to count your steps soon . . . unfortunately, you're still as young as ever to me, while I'm turning gray; but, since we're just as old, you can see in me how you're beginning to age . . .

WIFE: That's what you're waiting for!

HUSBAND: Yes! I've often wished you were old and ugly, that you had had smallpox, lost your teeth, just so I could keep you for myself and see an end to this anguish that never lets go of me!

WIFE: Lovely! And when you really had me old and ugly, you'd be calm until something else came up to be anxious about, and I'd have to sit there alone.

HUSBAND: No!

WIFE: Yes! Because I've noticed your love turns quite cool as soon as you have no reason to be jealous. Just remember last summer when we lived on an island where there were no other people. You were gone all day, fished, hunted, worked up a good appetite, got fat . . . and took on a confidence in your behavior which was almost insulting.

HUSBAND: And still, I remember, I was jealous—of the yard man!

WIFE: Good heavens!

HUSBAND: Well, I noticed you had quite a talk with him whenever you gave him an order, that you asked about his health, his prospects, and his love life before you sent him on to split wood . . . Why, you're blushing!

WIFE: Because of being ashamed of my husband . . .

HUSBAND: . . . who . . .

WIFE: . . . hasn't any shame!

HUSBAND: Well, you can say that like so many other things, but will you explain why you hate me?

WIFE: I've never hated you; I've just despised you! Why? Most likely for the same reason I despise all men, as soon as they—what's it called? love me. That's how it is, I don't know why.

HUSBAND: I've noticed that's how it is, so I've wanted to be able to hate you above everything else so you could love me. Pity the man who loves his wife!

WIFE: Poor you, and poor me! What can we do about it?

HUSBAND: Nothing! We've gone here and there for seven years, I with the hope chance would bring something to change this! I've even tried to fall in love with someone else but haven't succeeded. In the meanwhile your constant contempt and my eternal absurdity have robbed me of courage, faith in myself and in my ability to act. I've left you six times—and now I'm going to try a seventh time! (*Gets up and picks up the bag.*)

WIFE: So they were attempts to run away, your little trips by yourself?

HUSBAND: Failures every one of them! Last time I got to

Genoa. I went to museums but didn't see any paintings, only you; I went to the opera, heard no opera singers, only your voice in every nuance; got into a Pompeian cafe, and the only woman who appealed to me was like you, or became like you!

WIFE (*indignantly*): Did you go to places like that?

HUSBAND: Yes, that's how far my love led me, and my virtue, which embarrassed me, because it made me ridiculous.

WIFE: You know, now everything's over between us!

HUSBAND: I imagine it is since you never can be jealous of me.

WIFE: No, I've never felt that sickness, not even about Rosa, who's madly in love with you.

HUSBAND: How ungrateful of me not to have noticed that! On the other hand, I have had suspicions of the old baroness when she has so many errands to that large cupboard; but since she's our landlady and the furniture is hers, I can have been mistaken about the nature of her motive for wandering in and out of these rooms . . .

I'll go get dressed; I'll be gone in half an hour—without saying good-bye if you don't mind!

WIFE: You're afraid of good-byes in general?

HUSBAND: And especially of saying good-bye to you, yes! (*Goes.*)

The WIFE *is alone for a moment; then* ROSA *comes in, carelessly dressed, with her hair down, a folded towel about her head, cheeks, and jaw, indicating she has a toothache; a hole has been torn in the left sleeve of her dress. She is carrying a large basket of flowers.*

WIFE: Rosa! How are you, child?

ROSA: Good morning, ma'am! My toothache's so bad I wish I were dead!

WIFE: Poor dear!

ROSA: And tomorrow I'm to be in the procession for the feast of Corpus Christi—and I was going to tie up the roses today. Mr. Brunner promised to help with that! Oh, my teeth hurt!

WIFE: Let me see if you have a cavity. Open wide! Oh, what teeth! Pearls, my dear child! (*Kisses* ROSA *on the mouth.*)

ROSA (*crossly*): You mustn't kiss me, ma'am! You mustn't! I don't want you to! (*She clambers up on the table and sits down with her feet on a chair.*) Besides I don't know what I want. I'd like to have been along at the party yesterday—but I had to stay home alone and do my lessons—lessons like a school child, and then sit on the same bench as those brats! But I don't let the captain hold me under my jaw any longer for I'm not a child! I'm not! And if Mother comes and pulls my hair, then . . . I don't know what I'll do to her!

WIFE: Rosa dear, what's wrong? What has happened?

ROSA: I don't know what it is, but my head and my teeth are throbbing; it feels as if I had a red-hot poker in my back—and life makes me sick. I'd like to drown myself, I'd like to run away, wander about at fairs and sing, be attacked by shameless men . . .

WIFE: Listen, Rosa! Listen to me!

ROSA: I'd like to have a baby—if it only weren't a disgrace to get a baby! (*Sighs. Catches sight of the bag.*) Who's going away?

WIFE: Why . . . my husband!

ROSA: Then you've been mean to him again! Ma'am! Where is he going? How far is he going? When will he come back?

WIFE: I don't know!

ROSA: So! And you haven't asked him? (*Looking through the contents of the bag.*) But I see that he intends to go far away for here is his passport! Far away! Far away? Why can't you be good to him, ma'am, who's so good to you! (*She throws herself into the* WIFE'S *arms and bursts into tears.*)

WIFE: Poor dear! You're crying, poor girl! Poor little innocent!

ROSA: I like Mr. Brunner so much!

WIFE: And you're not ashamed to say that to me, his wife! And I'm to comfort you, my little rival! Weep, child; it's good to be able to weep!

ROSA (*tears herself away*): No! If I don't want to, I don't cry, and if I want to pick up what you throw away, I'll do that! I don't ask anyone for permission to like anyone or anything I want!

WIFE: Well, well! But are you sure he likes you?

ROSA (*back in the* WIFE's *arms; weeping*): No, I'm not!

WIFE (*tenderly, comfortingly*): Shall I ask him very nicely to like you! Shall I?

ROSA (*weeping*): Yes-s! But he mustn't go away! He mustn't! Be nice to him, ma'am, so he won't go!

WIFE: What am I to do, you crazy little child?

ROSA: I can't tell you! But let him kiss you as much as he wants to—oh, I saw you in the garden the other day when he wanted to and you didn't . . . and then I thought—

BARONESS (*enters*): Excuse my disturbing you, but, with your permission, I have to get in that cupboard!

WIFE (*gets up*): Feel absolutely free, Baroness!

BARONESS: Why, there's Rosa! Are you up? I thought you were sick in bed! Go do your lessons right away!

ROSA: There's the festival tomorrow so there's no school as you know very well, Mother.

BARONESS: Go anyway, and don't come in here and disturb our guests!

WIFE (*going toward the door at the back*): Rosa doesn't disturb us at all, and we're the best of friends . . . We were just about to go down into the garden to pick flowers . . . so we could try on the white dress she's going to wear tomorrow!

ROSA (*goes out at the back with a nod of secret understanding to the* WIFE): Thank you, ma'am!

BARONESS (*to the* WIFE): You're spoiling my Rosa thoroughly!

WIFE: A little friendliness doesn't spoil anyone, Baroness, least of all Rosa, who's a girl with a great heart and an exceptional mind.

The BARONESS *digs away in the cupboard; the* WIFE *stands in the doorway; the* HUSBAND *comes in through the left door; exchanges a look with his* WIFE, *whereupon they both smile as they observe the* BARONESS. *The* HUSBAND *is carrying a few packages which he puts into the bag; the* WIFE *leaves.*)

BARONESS: Excuse my disturbing you . . . but it'll take only a moment . . .

HUSBAND: Don't let it embarrass you, Baroness!

BARONESS (*comes up stage*): Are you leaving again, Mr. Brunner?

HUSBAND: Yes!

BARONESS: Are you taking a long trip?

HUSBAND: Perhaps! Perhaps not!

BARONESS: You don't know?

HUSBAND: I never really know what's ahead of me since I put my future in someone else's hand!

BARONESS: May I say something personal, Mr. Brunner?

HUSBAND: That depends! You're a good friend of my wife's?

BARONESS: As much as two women can be friends, yes! But my age, my knowledge of life, and my temperament . . . (*Stops herself.*) However . . . I have seen you're unhappy, and I've suffered in the same way as you, so I know your sickness can be healed only by years.

HUSBAND: Am I really the one who's sick? Isn't my behavior absolutely normal? And am I not really suffering from seeing the other one's abnormal—or sick?

BARONESS: . . . I was married to a man I loved . . . you smile—you don't think a woman can love, because . . .

but I did love him, and he loved me, too, but—he loved other women, too! So I suffered from jealousy, so, so . . . I became insufferable for him! He went to war; he was an officer, of course; but he never came back. They said he was killed, but his body was never found, and I imagine he's alive, united with another woman. Imagine, I'm still jealous of my dead husband! I dream at night that I see him with the other woman . . . Mr. Brunner, have you known that agony?

HUSBAND: Believe me, I have! But how did you get the idea he's still alive? (*Arranging things in his bag.*)

BARONESS: Of course I had had some suspicions, based on a great many contradictory circumstances, but the years went by without my getting any support for my notion. Then four months ago you people came—a strange chance made me notice there was a striking resemblance between you and my husband and I noticed it right away. It became a reminder, and when my fantasies got a visible form, my old doubts grew into a conviction, and now I believe he's alive; I'm tortured by this eternally consuming jealousy—that's why I've understood you.

HUSBAND (*who has listened to the first part of the* BARONESS' *explanation rather indifferently now becomes more and more attentive*): Your husband resembled me, you said . . . Please sit down, Baroness!

BARONESS (*sits down at the table, facing the audience; the* HUSBAND *sits beside her*): He looked like you, and his character, except for his weaknesses, was like yours, too . . .

HUSBAND: And he'd be about ten years older than I . . . and he had a scar as if from a needle on his right cheek . . .

BARONESS: Absolutely right!

HUSBAND: Then I ran into your husband one night in London!

BARONESS: He's still alive?

HUSBAND: I'll figure that out right now; at the moment I don't know! Let me see . . . that was five years ago . . . as I said, in London. I was in mixed company; our mood had been depressed; and on the way home I joined the first man I could talk things out with. We hit it off, so our conversation became a sidewalk conversation lasting for many hours—the man told me his whole story after he heard I came from the same area.

BARONESS: So he is alive?

HUSBAND: At least he didn't die in the war, for he was taken prisoner . . . fell in love with the mayor's daughter, fled to England, was deserted by her and began to gamble, and had bad luck. When we parted in the morning he impressed me as a lost soul. And he made me promise that if chance brought me into contact with you, after a year had gone by and he hadn't got word to me through an ad in the *Allgemeine Zeitung*, which I take, I could consider him dead. And when I met you, I was to kiss your hand for him and kiss your daughter's forehead, asking for forgiveness! (*He kisses the* BARONESS' *hand:* ROSA *appears at the back on the porch and observes what he does with wild looks.*)

BARONESS (*moved*): So he is dead!

HUSBAND: Yes! And I'd naturally have told you all this long since if both his name and the man had not slipped from my memory long ago!

(*The* BARONESS *twisting her handkerchief, hesitant.*)

HUSBAND: Do you feel calm now?

BARONESS: In a way! Yes! But there's a bit of hope, too!

HUSBAND: The hope of suffering still more of the sweet agony . . .

BARONESS: Perhaps! Aside from my child my anguish has been the only interest to fill my life—strange, that one should even miss the pain.

HUSBAND: I think—forgive me for saying it—you miss your jealousy more than you miss your husband!

BARONESS: Perhaps! My jealousy was the invisible bond which held me to this illusion. . . . But now that I haven't anything left . . . (*She takes the* HUSBAND's *hand.*) You, who brought me his last greeting, are like a living memory, and you, who have suffered the same way as I . . .

HUSBAND (*uneasy; gets up; looks at his watch*): Excuse me, but I must catch the next train! I must!

BARONESS: That's just what I intended to ask you not to do! Why go? Don't you like it here? (ROSA *goes away.*)

HUSBAND: I've had some of my best hours during these stormy years in your house—I'm leaving with great regret—but I must . . .

BARONESS: Because of what happened last night?

HUSBAND: Not entirely . . . that was the last straw . . . excuse me, now I'll pack! (*Busy with his bag.*)

BARONESS: If you won't change your mind . . . Mayn't I help you since no one else wants to . . .

HUSBAND: Thank you, Baroness, but I'm almost finished . . . and do make our good-bye short so it doesn't get painful . . . your kindness to me has been a great comfort in my suffering, and it's as painful for me to leave you . . . (*The* BARONESS *is touched.*) as from a good mother! I saw sympathy in your eyes when tact kept you from saying it, and I thought I noticed occasionally your good influence on my family's happiness . . . when your age let you say something a younger woman's unwilling to hear from someone her own age . . .

BARONESS (*hesitantly*): Permit me to tell you then that your wife is no longer young . . .

HUSBAND: She is, to me!

BARONESS: But not to the world!

HUSBAND: Fine if that were so, but on the other hand her

coquetry gets more and more repulsive, the less her pretentions correspond to her good qualities, and the minute they'd laugh at her . . .

BARONESS: They already do!

HUSBAND: Really? Poor Olga! (*Thoughtful; then when the church bells strike the hour, he pulls himself together*): It's time! I'm leaving in half an hour!

BARONESS: But you can't go without having had breakfast!

HUSBAND: I'm not hungry—besides I'm already so upset because of traveling my nerves are trembling like telephone wires in frost . . .

BARONESS: Then I'll make you a cup of coffee—I may, mayn't I? And I'll send up the maid to help you pack!

HUSBAND: You're so very kind, Baroness, I could be tempted into weaknesses I'd regret!

BARONESS: You wouldn't regret taking my advice—if you only would! (*Goes.* ROSA *comes in at the back. Then the* MAID.)

HUSBAND: Good morning, Miss Rosa! How are you?

ROSA: Why?

HUSBAND: Why? Why, you have your head bandaged!

ROSA (*jerks off the bandage and stuffs it into her pocket*): Nothing wrong with me! I feel fine! So you're going away!

HUSBAND: Yes, I'm going away!

ROSA (*to the* MAID): What do you want?

MAID: The baroness told me to help Mr. Brunner pack!

ROSA: You don't need to! Just go! (*The* MAID *leaves, hesitantly.*) Go, I say!

HUSBAND: Are you being impolite to me, Miss Rosa?

ROSA: No, I'm not! I want to help you, myself! But you're impolite—you promised to help me with the flowers for tomorrow's festival! I don't care about that, for . . . I'm not going to any festival tomorrow, for . . . I don't know where I'll be tomorrow!

HUSBAND: What do you mean?

ROSA: May I help you with something, Mr. Brunner? May I brush your hat? (*She takes his hat and brushes it.*)

HUSBAND: I can't let you do that, Miss Rosa! (*He tries to take his hat away from her.*)

ROSA: No, let me be! There, you tore my dress! (*She puts her fingers into the hole in the sleeve and rips the sleeve.*)

HUSBAND: Miss Rosa, you're very strange today—I think you're upsetting your mother with your strange behavior.

ROSA: What do I care if she's upset? That would really amuse me though it would make you sad, perhaps; but I don't care about you any more than about the cat in the kitchen or the rat in the cellar, and if I were your wife, I'd despise you and go so far away you could never find me again! Shame, kissing another woman! Shame!

HUSBAND: So, child, you saw me kiss your mother's hand. That was a last greeting from your father whom I ran into abroad after you saw him last. And I even have a greeting for you . . . (*He goes up to her, takes her head between his hands and wants to kiss her forehead, but* ROSA *throws back her head and presses her lips against his mouth. Just then the* WIFE *appears on the porch, is startled by what she sees, and goes.*) Rosa, my child, I intended to give you an innocent kiss on the forehead!

ROSA: Innocent! (*Laughs.*) Very innocent! And you believe Mother's stories about Father, who died several years ago! He was a man who could love, who dared to love! He didn't tremble because of a kiss and he didn't wait for an invitation! If you don't believe me, come along to the attic and I'll let you read his letters to the women he loves—come on! (*She opens the wallpapered door so that the attic stairs can be seen. Laughs.*) You're afraid I'll seduce you, and you look amazed. Amazed that I, a mere girl, who has been a woman for three years knows that love isn't innocent! Do you imagine I believe children are born through the ear? Now you despise me, I see, but you shouldn't, for I'm no worse and no better than the rest . . .

HUSBAND: Miss Rosa! Go change your dress, before your mother comes!

ROSA: Do you think my arms are that ugly! Or don't you dare look at them! Now I'll soon understand why your wife . . . why you're jealous of your wife!

HUSBAND: This is going pretty far!

ROSA: You're blushing . . . for me or for yourself? Do you know how many times I've been in love?

HUSBAND: Not once!

ROSA: Not once with a shy man, no! Now you despise me again, don't you?

HUSBAND: Yes, a little! Protect your heart, Miss Rosa, and don't wear it on your sleeve to be hacked away at—and to be soiled! You're a woman, you say, but you're a very young woman, what people call a girl . . .

ROSA: So, and so . . . but I can become a young woman . . .

HUSBAND: But since you're not one yet . . . we'll postpone this kind of talk until then! Shake hands on that, Miss Rosa!

ROSA (*crying because she is furious*): Never! Never! You!

HUSBAND: Can't we part as friends? We who have had so many good days together this sad winter and long spring? (*His* WIFE *comes in with a coffee tray. She is somewhat embarrassed and pretends not to notice* ROSA.)

WIFE: I thought you'd have time for a cup of warm coffee before you left!

ROSA *wants to take the tray away from the* WIFE.)

WIFE: Thank you, dear, I'll do it!

HUSBAND (*observing his wife with wondering, somewhat ironic, looks*): That's a good idea . . .

WIFE (*without looking him in the eyes*): I'm glad . . . that . . .

ROSA: Maybe I may say good-bye now . . . to Mr. Brunner . . .

HUSBAND: Are you going to leave me now, Miss Rosa . . .

ROSA: Yes, I suppose I'd better . . . now . . . that your wife's angry at me!

WIFE: I? No, Miss . . .

ROSA: You promised to help me try on my dress . . .

WIFE: Not just now, child, when I'm busy . . . or perhaps you want to keep my husband company while I go check on it . . .

HUSBAND: Olga! . . .

WIFE: Yes?

    ROSA *fingers in her mouth, embarrassed, angry.*)

WIFE: Go get dressed properly, Miss, if you're going with him to the train! (ROSA *as before.*) And take your flowers with you in case there's a question of throwing them . . .

HUSBAND: You are cruel, Olga!

ROSA (*curtsies*): Good-bye, Mr. Brunner!

HUSBAND: (*takes Rosa's hand*): Good-bye, Miss Rosa, have a good life, and become a big girl, a really big girl soon!

ROSA (*takes her flowers*): Good-bye, Mrs. Brunner! (*The* WIFE *does not answer.*) Good-bye! (*Runs out. Both* HUSBAND *and* WIFE *are embarrassed—the* WIFE *avoids looking directly at her* HUSBAND.)

WIFE: Can I help you with anything?

HUSBAND: No, I'm almost ready!

WIFE: You have so many to help you anyway!

HUSBAND: May I look at you? (*He tries to take her head between his hands.*)

WIFE (*tears herself away*): No, let me be!

HUSBAND: What is this?

WIFE: You probably think . . . I'm jealous?

HUSBAND: Now I do, when you say it, but I couldn't believe it before.

WIFE: And with a school girl like that! Ugh!

HUSBAND: The object doesn't seem to matter in cases like this; why, I've been jealous of a yard man! So you saw . . .

WIFE: That you kissed her!

HUSBAND: No, she kissed me!

WIFE: Shameless! But hussies like that are like apes!

HUSBAND: They do what they see grownups do!

WIFE: You seem delighted by her attentions in any case . . .

HUSBAND: . . . unused as I am to such attentions . . .

WIFE: From young women, maybe . . . you seem to be less afraid of older ones . . .

HUSBAND: So you saw that, too?

WIFE: No, but Rosa told me! So you're a real lady's man!

HUSBAND: I must be! It's a shame I can't profit from it!

WIFE: You'll soon be free to choose a younger and prettier wife!

HUSBAND: No, I won't be free to do that!

WIFE: For I'm old and ugly now!

HUSBAND: What has happened? Let me look at you once more! (*He approaches her.*)

WIFE: (*putting her head down on his chest*): No, you mayn't look at me!

HUSBAND: What in the world is this? Surely you're not jealous of a schoolgirl or an old widow . . .

WIFE: I've broken . . . a front tooth! Don't look at me!

HUSBAND: Child! You got your first tooth in pain and lost your first tooth in sorrow!

WIFE: And now you'll desert me!

HUSBAND: No! (*Closes his bag.*) Tomorrow we'll both go to Augsburg to get you a gold tooth!

WIFE: But we'll never come back here!

HUSBAND: Never, if that's what you want!

WIFE: And you're satisfied now?

HUSBAND: Yes—for eight days! (*The* BARONESS *comes in with a tray.*)

BARONESS: (*embarrassed*): Excuse me, I thought . . .

HUSBAND: Thank you, Baroness, I've already had coffee, but for your sake I'll have another cup! And if you . . . (ROSA *appears in the doorway wearing her white dress.*) and if Miss Rosa would join us we'd like that . . . we'd like it especially since I and my wife are leaving on the first train tomorrow!

[CURTAIN]

Facing Death

A Tragedy

Characters

DURAND, *proprietor of a boardinghouse, formerly an employee of the National Railways*

ADÉLE, *his daughter, 27*

ANNETTE, *his daughter, 24*

THÉRÈSE, *his daughter, 18*

ANTONIO, *a lieutenant in an Italian cavalry regiment*

Setting

In French Switzerland in the 1880s

A dining room with a long table. Through the open door at the back can be seen, above the tops of the churchyard's cypress trees, Lake Leman, the Savoy Alps and the French bathing resort Evian. To the left a door to the kitchen. To the right a door to the living quarters. DURAND *is standing looking out on the lake through binoculars.* ADÈLE *enters from the kitchen; she is wearing an apron, has her sleeves rolled up, and is carrying a coffee tray.*

ADÈLE: Haven't you gone out to get the coffee bread yet, Father?

DURAND: No, I sent Pierre. My chest has been so bad the last few days I can't walk up the steep hill.

ADÈLE: Pierre again! That'll cost three sous! Where'll we get them when there hasn't been more than one traveler in our house the last three months?

DURAND: That's very true but I think Annette could fetch the bread!

ADÈLE: That would ruin our credit completely, but then you've never done anything else!

DURAND: Even you, Adèle!

ADÈLE: Even I have tired, but I held out the longest!

DURAND: Yes, you did, and you were still human when Thérèse and Annette tortured me. You and I have kept the house going since Mother died. You had to sit in the kitchen like Cendrillon and I had to take care of the service, sweep, brush, fire, run errands. You're tired; what shouldn't I be then?

ADÈLE: But you mayn't be tired when you have three children who are unprovided for and whose dowry you've destroyed!

DURAND (*listening to something outside*): Aren't they ringing bells and beating drums down toward Cully? If fire has broken out, they're lost—the Föhn'll soon be blowing—I see that on the lake.

ADÈLE: Have you paid the fire insurance on our house?

DURAND: Yes, I have; otherwise, I wouldn't have got the latest mortgage loan.

ADÈLE: How much is still unencumbered?

DURAND: A fifth of the fire insurance value. But you know how values fell when they put in the railroad past our gates.

ADÈLE: So much the better then! . . .

DURAND (*sternly*): Adèle! (*Pause*) Will you put out the fire in the stove?

ADÈLE: Can't before the coffee bread has come!

DURAND: Well, that's here now! (PIERRE *enters with a basket.*)

ADÈLE (*examines the basket*): No bread! Just a bill! Two, three of them!

PIERRE: Yes, the baker said he won't let you have any more until he's been paid. And as I went past the butcher's and the grocer's, they gave me these bills. (*Goes.*)

ADÈLE: God in heaven, now we're done for! But what's this? (*Opens a package.*)

DURAND: They're candles I've bought for a mass for my beloved René. You see, it's his deathday today.

ADÈLE: You can afford things like that!

DURAND: Out of my tips, yes. Don't you find it humiliating that I have to stick out my hand when travelers move out . . . Do you begrudge me the only satisfaction I have enjoying my sorrow, once a year! To live in the memory of the most beautiful thing life has given me.

ADÈLE: If he were alive right now, you'd find out how fine he was!

DURAND: Very likely your skepticism has something to it . . . the way I remember him, he wasn't like the rest of you!

ADÈLE: Please wait on Mr. Antonio yourself when he comes to drink coffee and there isn't any bread! If Mother were only alive! She always had the knack of managing when you stood there helpless.

DURAND: Your mother had her good points!

ADÈLE: But you saw only bad ones!

DURAND: Mr. Antonio's coming! If you step out, I'll talk to him!

ADÈLE: It'd be better if you went out and borrowed money so scandal could be avoided!

DURAND: I can't borrow a sou! After having borrowed for ten years! Let it all collapse at once, everything, just so it'll be over!

ADÈLE: Over for you, yes! But you never think of us!

DURAND: No, I have never thought of you! Never!

ADÈLE: Are you dunning us for our bringing up again?

DURAND: Only answering an unjustified complaint! Go now, I'll meet the storm as usual!

ADÈLE: As usual! Hm! (*Goes.* ANTONIO *enters at the back.*)

ANTONIO: Good morning, Mr. Durand.

DURAND: You've already been out for a walk, Lieutenant?

ANTONIO: Yes, I was down at Cully and looked on while they put out a chimney fire! So it'll be good to have my coffee!

DURAND: I needn't tell you how painful to have to admit we can no longer stay open because of lack of funds.

ANTONIO: How so?

DURAND: Putting it bluntly, we're bankrupt!

ANTONIO: But, my dear Mr. Durand, isn't there some

possibility of helping you out of this temporary embarrassment?

DURAND: No, there's no possibility, and the position of our business has been so thoroughly undermined for several years I'd rather see it collapse than have to worry day and night over what must come!

ANTONIO: But I still think you take too dark a view!

DURAND: On what grounds do you dare to doubt my statement?

ANTONIO: Because I want to help you.

DURAND: I don't want any help! Need must come to teach my children to lead another kind of life than this one which is simply play. With the exception of Adèle who really manages the kitchen, what do they do? Play and sing, take walks and flirt; and as long as there's a piece of bread in the house, they don't do anything useful!

ANTONIO: That may be, but while your financial situation is being cleared up, we have to have food in the house. Let me stay another month and I'll pay my bill in advance.

DURAND: No, thank you, because this thing has to be settled even if we end up in disaster. And I don't want to keep on with this business which doesn't bring in bread and butter but only humiliation. Think of last spring when we hadn't had a single paying guest for three months. Finally an American family arrived and saved us. The very next morning I saw their son on the stairs embracing my daughter—it was Thérèse—trying to kiss her. What would you have done in my place?

ANTONIO (*embarrassed*): I don't know . . .

DURAND: Well, I know what I should have done—but as her father, I didn't do it! Next time I know what I'll do!

ANTONIO: It seems to me that's why you should think of what you do and not leave your daughters to chance . . .

DURAND: Lieutenant . . . you're a young man, for whom I've

taken a liking for some reason or other. Whether this means anything to you or not, I ask you for one favor: Don't have any opinions at all about me or my behavior.

ANTONIO: I won't, Mr. Durand, if you'll only answer one question: Were you born in Switzerland?

DURAND: I'm a Swiss citizen!

ANTONIO: I know, but I asked if you were born in Switzerland?

DURAND: (*hesitantly*): Yes!

ANTONIO: I only asked, because—it interested me. But—since I have to believe you, when you say the house is to be closed, I want to pay my bill. It's only ten francs, but I can't leave without paying up.

DURAND: I'm not sure if this is right, for I don't keep the books, but if you've deceived me, you'll have to answer for it! Now I'll go to fetch bread. Then we'll see! (*Goes. Then* THÉRÈSE *carrying a rat trap and dressed in her bathrobe and with her hair down comes in.* ADÈLE *follows..*)

THÉRÈSE: Why, there's Antonio! I thought I heard the old man!

ANTONIO: Well, he went to get the coffee bread, he said!

THÉRÈSE: Hadn't he already done that? No, you know we can't have him about any longer!

ANTONIO: You're very pretty today, Thérèse, but that rat trap's not becoming to you.

THÉRÈSE: And what a trap it is. I've baited it for a whole month and not caught anything but the bait's been eaten every morning. Have you seen Mimmi?

ANTONIO: That damn cat? It's always in the way in here. But fortunately I've been spared today!

THÉRÈSE: You should speak kindly about the absent, and remember the one who loves me, loves my cat! (*Puts the rat trap on the table and picks up an empty saucer under the table.*) Adèle! Adèle!

ADÈLE (*appears in the door to the kitchen*): What are you ordering so loudly, Your Grace?

THÉRÈSE: I'm ordering milk for my cat, and a bit of cheese for your rats!

ADÈLE: Get them yourself!

THÉRÈSE: Is that an answer to Your Grace?

ADÈLE: Bluntly, yes! And you ought to be scolded for appearing before a stranger without having put up your hair!

THÉRÈSE: Why, he's only an old acquaintance, and . . . Antonio, speak nicely to Aunt Adèle so you'll get milk for Mimmi! (ANTONIO *hesitates.*) Well, aren't you going to obey?

ANTONIO (*sharply*): No!

THÉRÈSE: What's that? Do you want to feel the riding whip?

ANTONIO: Watch it!

THÉRÈSE (*perplexed*): What's this? What is this? Are you reminding me about my place, my guilt, and my weakness?

ANTONIO: No, I only wanted to remind you of my place, my guilt, and my weakness!

ADÈLE (*takes the cat's saucer*): Listen, my friends, what are you up to? Behave yourselves—and I'll bring you some good coffee. (*Goes into the kitchen.*)

THÉRÈSE (*weeping, to* ANTONIO): You're tired of me, Antonio, and you're thinking of abandoning me.

ANTONIO: Don't cry—it makes your eyes ugly.

THÉRÈSE: If they don't get as pretty as Annette's . . . then . . .

ANTONIO: So it's Annette now? Listen, all joking aside, it seems to me it's taking a long time to get that coffee . . .

THÉRÈSE: You'd make a pleasant husband who can't wait for a minute for his coffee.

ANTONIO: And what a lovable wife you'd be who couldn't do

something stupid without nagging at your husband. (ANNETTE *enters, dressed, her hair up.*)

ANNETTE: Why, you're quarreling in the morning!

ANTONIO: Look at Annette, already dressed!

THÉRÈSE: Yes, Annette's perfect in every way, and she has the advantage of being older than I . . .

ANNETTE: If you don't keep your mouth shut . . .

ANTONIO:. There! There! Behave yourself, Thérèse! (*He puts his arm about her waist and kisses her.* MR. DURAND *appears in the doorway. Stops, amazed.*)

DURAND: What is this?

THÉRÈSE: (*tears herself away from* ANTONIO): What?

DURAND: Can I believe my eyes?

THÉRÈSE: What did you see?

DURAND: I saw you let that man kiss you.

THÉRÈSE: That's a lie!

DURAND: Have I lost my sight or do you dare to lie to my face?

THÉRÈSE: Are you the one to talk about lying, you who lie to us and to everyone else that you're Swiss by birth though you are a Frenchman?

DURAND: Who said so?

THÉRÈSE: Mother did!

DURAND (*to* ANTONIO): Lieutenant, since you've paid your bill, I ask you to leave—immediately! Otherwise . . .

ANTONIO:. Otherwise?

DURAND: You may select the weapons!

ANTONIO:. I wonder what you'd select as weapon, aside from running away!

DURAND: If I didn't prefer my cane, I'd take my rifle from the last war . . .

THÉRÈSE: You've really been at war, you, who deserted!

DURAND: So Mother said that, too! I can't fight with a corpse but I can make someone a corpse! (*He lifts his thick stick and goes toward* ANTONIO. THÉRÈSE *and* ANNETTE *throw themselves between the two men.*)

ANNETTE: Think what you're doing!

THÉRÈSE: You'll end on the gallows!

ANTONIO (*going*): Good-bye, Mr. Durand! Keep my contempt and my ten francs!

DURAND (*takes a gold coin out of his vest pocket and throws it after* ANTONIO): May my curses go with your gold, you rascal!

THÉRÈSE *and* ANNETTE (to ANTONIO): Don't go, don't go! Father will kill us!

DURAND (*breaks his stick in two*): The one who can't kill dies!

ANTONIO:. Good-bye, and miss me, the last rat on the sinking ship! (*Leaves.*)

THÉRÈSE (*to* DURAND): That's how you treat our guests! Is it any wonder the place is going under?

DURAND: That's how. What guests!—But tell me, Thérèse, my child . . . (*He takes her head between his hands*) My dear child, tell me if I didn't see what I thought I saw just now, or if you were lying . . .

THÉRÈSE (*furiously*): What are you talking about?

DURAND: You know what I mean! And it isn't the thing itself, which can be rather innocent . . . Can I rely on my senses? That's what interests me.

THÉRÈSE: Talk about something else instead . . . tell us what we're going to eat and drink today! Besides, it's a lie he kissed me!

DURAND: It's not a lie! In heaven's name, I saw it happen!

THÉRÈSE: Prove it!

DURAND: Prove it! With two witnesses or a policeman! (*To* ANNETTE) Annette, my child, will you tell me the truth?

ANNETTE: I didn't see anything!

DURAND: That's the right answer—you shouldn't tell on your sister. How like your mother you are today, Annette!

ANNETTE: Don't say anything against Mother! She should have lived to see a day like this! (ADÈLE *enters with a glass of milk which she puts on the table.*)

ADÈLE (*to* DURAND): There's your milk! How did it go with the bread?

DURAND: I didn't get any bread, children, but things will go on as they've gone.

THÉRÈSE (*snatches the glass of milk from her father*): You're not going to have anything, you who throw away the money so your children can starve.

ADÈLE: Did he throw away the money, that wretch? He should have been put into the insane asylum that time Mother said he was ready for it! Here's another bill that came by way of the kitchen!

DURAND *looks at the bill; is startled; pours a glass of water, drinks it; sits down and lights his pipe.*)

ANNETTE: But smoke tobacco, you can afford that?

DURAND (*weary and resigned*): This tobacco hasn't cost you more than water—I got it as a gift half a year ago! So don't get upset unnecessarily.

THÉRÈSE (*takes away the matches*): But at least you're not going to waste matches . . .

DURAND: If you knew, Thérèse, how many matches I've wasted because of you, when I had to get up nights to see you hadn't kicked off your blankets; if you, Annette, knew how many times I've given you water, when you were screaming from thirst, but your mother had the conviction it was bad for children to drink water.

THÉRÈSE: That was long ago so I don't care about that. Besides it was only your duty as you've said yourself!

DURAND: Yes, it was, and I did it! And a bit more besides!

ADÈLE: Keep on doing that! Otherwise no one will know what's to become of us! Three young girls left without care and protection, without any means for living. Do you know what necessity can drive us to?

DURAND: I said that ten years ago, but no one wanted to listen to me; twenty years ago I said this moment would come, but I haven't been able to prevent it from coming. I've sat like a single brakeman on an express train, seen how it's going to crash, but I haven't been able to get at the controls to stop it.

THÉRÈSE: And now you expect our thanks for wrecking it with us on board!

DURAND: No, child, I'm simply asking you to be a little less nasty toward me. You have cream for the cat, but you begrudge milk for your father, who hasn't [really] eaten . . . for a long time.

THÉRÈSE: So it's you who have begrudged a little milk for the cat!

DURAND: Yes, it's I!

ANNETTE: And maybe you've eaten up the rat bait, too?

DURAND: Yes!

ADÈLE: What a pig!

THÉRÈSE (*laughs*): Imagine if it had been poisoned!

DURAND: If it only had been, you mean!

THÉRÈSE: Yes, surely you wouldn't have had anything against that, you who have always been chattering about shooting yourself but haven't done it!

DURAND: Why haven't I shot myself? That *is* a blunt accusation! Well, do you know why I haven't? So you wouldn't have to drown yourselves, my dear children! Say something else that's nasty! For me that's like hearing music, well-known melodies from . . . the good old days . . .

ADÈLE: Quit that talk, which is pointless and doesn't get anywhere! Do something!

THÉRÈSE: Do you know what will happen to us if you leave us like this?

DURAND: You'll become prostitutes, I suppose. That's what your mother always said, when she had spent the household money on lottery tickets.

ADÈLE: Keep still! And not one word about our dear, beloved mother

DURAND (*muttering to himself*): A candle's burning; in this house; and when it has burned down, my objective will have been won. I suppose you'd say won! And then the wind will come with a great roar! Yes! No! (*The wind has begun to blow outside, and it is becoming cloudy.* DURAND *jumps up; says to* ADÈLE) Put out the fire in the stove! The great wind is coming!

ADÈLE (*looks* DURAND *in the eye*): No great wind is coming!

DURAND: Put out the fire in the stove! If it spreads from there we won't get any insurance. Put out the fire, I say! Put it out!

ADÈLE: I don't understand you!

DURAND (*looks her in the eye and takes her hands*): Just obey me! Do as I say! (ADÈLE *goes out into the kitchen; she leaves the door open.* DURAND *to* THÉRÈSE *and* ANNETTE) Go up and shut your windows, children, and see to the dampers! But give me a kiss first for I'm going to take a trip—to get money for you!

THÉRÈSE: Can you get money?

DURAND: I have life insurance I'm thinking of turning in.

THÉRÈSE: How much will you get for it?

DURAND: Six hundred francs if I sell it, and five thousand if I die. (THÉRÈSE *embarrassed.*) Speak up, child! No? We're not to be cruel unnecessarily. Tell me, Thérèse, do you like

Antonio so much you'll be quite unhappy if you don't get him?

THÉRÈSE: Oh yes!

DURAND: Then you ought to marry him if he loves you, that is! But don't be mean to him for then you'll be unhappy! Good-bye, my dear child! (*Embraces her and kisses her on the cheeks.*)

THÉRÈSE: You mustn't die, Father! You mustn't!

DURAND: Do you begrudge me peace?

THÉRÈSE: Not if you want it! Forgive me, Father, for all the times I've been unkind to you.

DURAND: Not worth mentioning, child!

THÉRÈSE: But no one was as unkind to you as I!

DURAND: I noticed it less, for I loved you most—why, I don't know. There, there, go close the windows.

THÉRÈSE: Here are the matches, Father! And—your milk!

DURAND (*smiling*): Child, child!

THÉRÈSE: Well, what shall I do? I haven't anything else to give you.

DURAND: You gave me so much joy as a child that you don't owe me anything. Go now! And give me only a friendly look as you used to!

(THÉRÈSE *going, turns back, and throws herself into his arms.*)

DURAND: There, there, child, now everything's fine! (THÉRÈSE *runs out.*) Good-bye, Annette!

ANNETTE: Are you going away? I don't understand all this.

DURAND: I'm going away.

ANNETTE: But you'll come back, won't you, Father?

DURAND: No one knows if he'll be alive tomorrow, and in any case we can say good-bye.

ANNETTE: Good-bye then, Father! Have a good trip! You won't forget to bring something home for us, as you used to? (*Going.*)

DURAND: So you remember that, though it's long since I bought anything for you children! Good-bye, Annette! (*To himself, softly*) For good and evil, for big and small, and where you've sowed, others will reap! (ADÈLE *enters.*) Adèle! Now you're going to listen to me! And understand! That I speak discreetly simply means I want to spare your conscience from knowing too much. Take it easy; I have the others up in their rooms. I want you to ask me this first: "Do you have any life insurance?" Well-l!

ADÈLE (*uncertain, curious*): "Do you have any life insurance?"

DURAND: No, I did have a policy, but I sold it a long time ago because I thought I noticed someone was impatient about collecting on it. But I do have fire insurance! Here is the policy! Hide it carefully! Now I'll ask you: Do you know how many candles there are in a pound of candles for a mass at seventy-five centimes?

ADÈLE: Six!

DURAND (*pointing at the package of candles*): How many candles are left in that?

ADÈLE: Only five!

DURAND: Because the sixth one is very high up and very close!

ADÈLE: Good Lord!

DURAND (*takes up his watch*): In five minutes or so it will have burned down!

ADÈLE: No!

DURAND: Yes! Can you see any other daylight in this darkness? No! So! This about finances. Now another matter! That Mr. Durand leaves this world as an (*whispers*) arsonist doesn't matter, but that he has lived up to now as a man of honor his children should know. Well, I was born in France—I didn't have to admit that to the first rascal to come along. Just before I reached conscription age I fell in love with the girl who later became my wife. To get

married we moved here and became Swiss citizens! When
the latest war broke out and it looked as if I might have to
take up arms I enlisted as a volunteer sharpshooter against
the Germans! I have never been a deserter—your mother
made up that story!

ADÈLE: My mother never lied!

DURAND: There you are! The corpse is back again standing
between us. I cannot sue the dead, but I swear I'm telling
the truth! Listen! And about your dowry, that's to say
through your mother, the truth is this: Your mother
wasted—through   extravagance   and   stupid
speculations—what I had gotten through my father so
thoroughly I had to give up my job and set up this
boardinghouse. And part of her inheritance had to be used
for bringing you three up and that can't be called wasted, I
hope. So that, too, is untrue . . .

ADÈLE: But mother didn't put it like that on her
deathbed . . .

DURAND: Then your mother lied on her deathbed just as she
did her whole life through . . . And that's the curse that
has followed me like a ghost! Think how you've tortured
me with these two lies for so many years. I didn't want to
upset and disturb you when you were young and make
you doubt your mother's perfection, so I kept still. I was
her beast of burden through our whole married life; I bore
all her faults on my back, took the results of all her
mistakes on myself, until I finally thought I was the guilty
one. And she wasn't slow about believing herself blameless
first and then the victim! "Blame me," I used to say, when
she had got herself really involved in trouble. And she
blamed me! And I bore it! But the more she owed me, the
more she hated me with the whole boundless hatred of
gratitude, and finally she despised me in order to
strengthen herself by imagining she had fooled me! And

last of all she taught you girls to despise me, too, for she needed support in her weakness! I believed and hoped that wicked but weak soul would die when she died; but evil lives on and grows as sickness, while what is sound stops at a certain point to go down later. And when I wanted to change what was wrong in the ways of this house, then I met your "Mother"—"that's what Mother said" and therefore it's true: "Mother used to do it like that," so that was the right way. And to the three of you, I became a weakling when I was good, a wretch when I was sensitive, a scoundrel when you got your way and you ruined the house!

ADÈLE: It's nice to accuse a dead person, who can't defend herself!

DURAND (*speaks very rapidly, extremely excited*): I'm still not dead, but I will be soon! Will you defend me then? No, you don't need to! But defend your sisters. Think only of my children, Adèle. Look after Thérèse as a mother would. She's the youngest and the most lively, quick to evil and good, thoughtless, but weak! See to it she gets married soon if you can arrange it! Now, it smells as if straw were burning!

ADÈLE: The Lord preserve us!

DURAND (*drinking out of the water glass*): He will! And find a place as teacher for Annette! Then she'll get out into the world and be in good company. When the money comes, you're to take charge of it. Don't be stingy, but set your sisters up so they'll be presentable! Don't save anything but the family papers lying in my bureau, the middle drawer. Here's the key. You have the fire insurance policy. (*Smoke can be seen forcing its way through the ceiling*) Now it will soon be fulfilled! In a moment the bells of St. François Church will ring! Promise me one thing. Never tell this to your sisters! It would only upset them for life. (*He sits down by the table.*) And one more thing: never a bad word about their mother! Her portrait's in the bureau—you never got to know that—I thought it was enough to have her invisible spirit walking again in our home! Tell Thérèse she's to forgive me! Don't forget to see to it she gets the best when you buy her clothes—you know her weakness for things like that and where her weakness can lead her! Tell Annette. . . . (*A soft peal can be heard from outside. The smoke grows thicker.* MR. DURAND *rests his head in his arms on the table.*)

ADÈLE: It's burning! It's burning! Father—What's wrong? You'll be burned alive!

   (DURAND *raises his head and pushes the glass aside with a gesture full of meaning.*)

ADÈLE: You have . . . swallowed . . . poison!

DURAND (*nods in agreement*): Do you have the fire insurance policy? Tell Thérèse . . . and Annette . . . (*He puts his head down again. The bell tolls once more—noise and commotion offstage.*)

[CURTAIN]

Pariah

One Act

(A FREE DRAMATIZATION OF AN OLA HANSSON STORY)

Characters

MR. X, *a middle-aged archaeologist*

MR. Y, *a middle-aged traveler from America*

Setting

A simple room in the country; a door and a window with a view of the countryside. In the middle of the room a large dining-room table with books, writing utensils, artifacts on one side; microscopes, boxes of insects, alcohol jars on the other.

To the right a bookshelf. Otherwise the furniture is that of a rich farmer.

MR. Y, *in his shirtsleeves, comes in with a butterfly net and vasculum; goes directly to the bookshelf and takes down a book which he puts on the table to read.*

The bells from the country church can be heard ringing at the end of services; the landscape and the cottage are drenched in sunlight.

Now and then clucking of chickens outside can be heard. MR. X *enters, in shirt sleeves.* MR. Y *is violently startled, puts the book back upside down; pretends to be looking for another book.*

MR. X: What stifling heat! I'm sure there'll be thunder!

MR. Y: Really! Why do you think so?

MR. X: The bells are ringing so heavily, the flies stinging, and the chickens cackling. I was going fishing but couldn't find one worm. Don't you feel nervous?

MR. Y (*taking thought*): I?—Oh yes-s!

MR. X: You're always looking out as if you expected stormy weather as far as that goes!

MR. Y (*visibly startled*): I do?

MR. X: Well, since you're leaving tomorrow, too, it's no wonder you have travel fever! What's new?—There's the mail! (*Picks up a letter from the table.*) I get palpitations every time I open a letter—only bills, bills! Have you ever been in debt?

MR. Y (*thinks about that*): No-o!

MR. X: Well, then you don't understand how it can feel when unpaid bills show up. (*Reads a letter.*) Rent unpaid—the

119

landlord's complaining—his wife's upset! And I'm up to
my elbows in gold!

(*Opens an iron-fitted box on the table; the two men sit down
beside it, one on each side.*)

See, here I have six thousand crowns worth in gold which I
dug up in fourteen days! This bracelet's worth the 350
crowns I need! And with the whole lot I could have a
brilliant career. Naturally I'd have sketches made and the
figures readied for my dissertation and then I'd print
it—and go away. Why do you think I don't do that?

MR. Y: I suppose you're afraid of being found out?

MR. X: Maybe that's part of it! But don't you think an
intelligent person like me would be able to manage it so it
wouldn't be found out? Why, I'm out there
alone—without witnesses—digging in the hills. What
would be so remarkable about stuffing a little into my own
pockets?

MR. Y: Yes, but disposing of it is probably the most
dangerous!

MR. X? Huh! I'd melt the whole lot down, of course, and then
mold ducats—with the right weight, of course—

MR. Y: Of course!

MR. X: You can surely understand that! If I did want to make
counterfeit coins, then—I wouldn't have to dig for gold
first! (*Pause.*) Anyhow it is strange; if someone else should
do what I can't bring myself to do, I'd acquit him, but I
can't acquit myself. I'd be able to give a brilliant speech in
defense of the thief, show that this gold was *res nullius* or
no one's when it was put in the ground during a time when
there was no law of ownership, that it didn't belong to
anyone but the first comer, since the landowner hadn't
counted it as part of his holdings, and so on!

MR. Y: And you could do this more easily, most likely,
if—hm—the thief hadn't stolen because of need but, for

example, out of mania for collecting, scientific interest, or ambition to possess a discovery. Isn't that right?

MR. X: You mean I'd not be able to acquit him if he stole because of need? Well, that's exactly the only reason the law doesn't excuse! That is simple theft!

MR. Y: And you wouldn't excuse it?

MR. X: Hm! Excuse it! I don't suppose I could when the law doesn't. And I must admit I'd find it hard to accuse a collector of theft if he picked up an artifact in someone else's earth if he didn't have it in his collection!

MR. Y: So vanity, ambition would excuse what need couldn't excuse?

MR. X: And all the same need should be the stronger, the only excuse. Well, that's how it is! I can't change that any more than I can change my will not to steal on any and every situation!

MR. Y: So you count it a great virtue that you can't—hm—steal!

MR. X: That's as irresistible for me as the desire to steal is in others—so it's no virtue. I can't, and they can't refrain!—You surely understand I don't lack the desire to possess this gold! Then why don't I take it? I can't! It's an inability, and a shortcoming isn't a virtue, of course. There! (*Closes the box.*)

(*Clouds have been moving in over the countryside and cut off the sunlight on the cottage occasionally. Now it becomes dark as if a thunderstorm were about to break.*)

MR. X: How stifling it is! I think we'll get a thunderstorm!

(MR. Y *gets up and closes the doors and windows.*)

MR. X: Oh, are you afraid of thunder?

MR. Y: One should be careful! (*They sit down at the table again.*)

MR. X: You're a strange fellow! Here you dropped down like a bomb fourteen days ago, presented yourself as a

Swedish–American, who's collecting flies for a little museum—

MR. Y: Don't bother about me!

MR. X: That's what you always say when I get tired of talking about myself and want to pay some attention to you. That's probably why I took to you—you let me talk so much about myself! We became old acquaintances right away, you didn't have any rough edges I could bump into, no needles that stung. There was something so soft about your whole being, you were so considerate as only the most civilized people can be; you never were loud when you came home late, made no noise when you got up in the morning, overlooked minor matters, gave in when it looked like a confrontation—in a word, you were the perfect friend to be with! But you were absolutely too deferential, absolutely too negative, too quiet, that I wouldn't speculate about it—and you're so full of fear and dread—it looks as if you were a ghost or someone's double. You know, when I sit here in front of the mirror and look at your back—it's as if I saw someone else!

(MR. Y *turns and looks into the mirror.*)

MR. X: Well, you can't see your own back! From in front you look like an open-hearted man who's going toward his destiny, but from the back—well, I don't want to be impolite—but you do look as if you were carrying a burden, as if you were shying away from a whip lash, and when I see your red suspenders crossing each other against your white shirt . . . then it looks like a big label, a good label on a packing case . . .

MR. Y (*gets up*): I think I'll choke—if the thunder doesn't break out soon!

MR. X: It'll soon be here; just take it easy!—And your neck! It looks as if another face were there, but a face of a type

other than yours! You're so terribly narrow between the
ears, so I sometimes wonder, what race you belong to!
(*Lightning.*) That looked as if it struck at the sheriff's!

MR. Y (*uneasy*): At the sheriff's!

MR. X: Well, it only looked as if it did! But we won't get any
of that stormy weather! So sit down, and let's talk, since
you're leaving tomorrow.—

It's strange that you, whom I became friendly with
immediately, belong to those people whose faces I can't
recall when they're absent. When you're out in the field
and I think of you, I always get the image of another
acquaintance, who really doesn't look like you, but with
whom you share certain similarities.

MR. Y: Who's that?

MR. X: I don't want to say! But for several years I ate dinner
at the same place and there met a little blond man with
light, tortured eyes. He had an unbelievable ability to get
into the biggest crowd without elbowing anyone or being
elbowed; although he'd stand by the door, he could always
take a slice of bread three feet away; he always looked
happy being among people, and when he'd catch sight of
an acquaintance, he'd laugh loudly with delight, embrace,
and caress him as if he hadn't run into a human being for
years. If anyone stepped on his toes, he'd smile as if he
were asking to be excused for being in the way.

I saw him for two years and had fun guessing his
occupation and character, but I never asked anyone who
he was, because I didn't want to know, since my fun could
then stop.

That man had the same faculty as you—being impossible
to classify. Sometimes I thought he was a substitute
teacher, a noncommissioned officer, a pharmacist, an
assistant secretary in some government office, or a secret

policeman, and he seemed like you to be knocked together of two different pieces, because his front didn't fit with his back.

One day I read in the paper about a major forgery by a well-known civil bureaucrat.—I then learned my nondescript fellow had been the partner of the forger's brother and his name was Strawman; and then I found that Strawman had had a loan library, but that he's a police reporter for a big newspaper now. How could I find any connection between forgery, police, and the nondescript fellow's manner? I don't know, but I asked a friend if Strawman was punished and he answered neither yes nor no—he didn't know! (*Pause.*)

MR. Y: Well, was he—punished?

MR. X: No, he was not punished! (*Pause.*)

MR. Y: You think that was why he was strongly drawn to the police and was so afraid of offending people?

MR. X: Yes!

MR. Y: Did you see him afterwards?

MR. X: No, I didn't want to. (*Pause.*)

MR. Y: Would you have looked him up if he had been—punished?

MR. X: Yes, gladly!

    (MR. Y *gets up, takes a few steps.*)

MR. X: Sit still!—Why can't you sit still!

MR. Y: Where did you get this broadminded view of human situations? Are you a Christian?

MR. X: No, you can surely hear that I'm not!

MR. Y (*grimaces*).

MR. X: The Christian demands forgiveness, but I demand punishment in order to make things equal or whatever you want to call it! And you, who have been *locked up*, ought to know that.

MR. Y (*stops, uneasy, looks at Mr. X, first with wild, hate-filled*

eyes, then with amazement and admiration): How—can—you
—know—that?

MR. X: Why, I can see it!

MR. Y: How? How can you see it?

MR. X: I've learned! That's an art, too, as so many others! But
now we won't talk about that matter! (*Looks at his watch,
puts a paper to be signed on the table, dips the pen, and hands it
to* MR. Y.) I have to think about my shaky affairs. Please
witness my signature on this note I'm going to hand in at a
Malmö bank tomorrow when I go with you.

MR. Y: I don't intend to go by way of Malmö!

MR. X: No?

MR. Y: No!

MR. X: But you can sign the note anyway.

MR. Y: No-o!—I never sign any papers—

MR. X: —anymore! That's the fifth time you've refused to
write your name! The first time was on a postal
receipt—that's when I started to watch you; and I've
noticed you're terrified of taking hold of a pen! You
haven't sent a letter since you came except for a card, and
you wrote that with a pencil. Don't you understand I've
figured out your misstep!

Further! It's the seventh time I suppose you've refused
to go along to Malmö—you haven't been there once since
you came. Yet you came here from America just to see
Malmö. And you walk three miles south every morning to
the miller's hill to see the roofs in Malmö! And when you
stand there by the right window and look through the third
pane to the left from below, you can see the spires on the
castle and the chimneys of the provincial prison.

You see it's not I who's so bright but you who are so
stupid!

MR. Y: You despise me!

MR. X: No!

MR. Y: Yes, you do, you must!

MR. X: No!—See here's my hand!

(MR. Y *kisses the extended hand.*)

MR. X (*jerks his hand away*): What nonsense is that?

MR. Y: Forgive me but you're the first person to give me his hand after finding out—

MR. X: And now you don't want to be friends any longer!—It frightens me that after serving your sentence you don't consider yourself rehabilitated, on the same level as anyone else! Do you want to tell me what happened? Do you?

MR. Y (*squirming*): Yes, but you won't believe what I'll say; I'll tell you, and you'll see I'm no *ordinary* criminal. You'll be convinced that there are crimes which are, so to speak, unintentional (*squirming*)—which come of themselves—spontaneously—without free will, and that one's not to blame for! May I open the door a little? I think the stormy weather's over!

MR. X: Go ahead!

MR. Y (*opens the door, then sits down at the table and tells the following with dry enthusiasm, theatrical gestures, and false accents*): Well! You see! I was a student at Lund and was going to take out a bank loan. I didn't have any great debts and my father had a little property—not much, of course! But I had sent the promissory note to the second person for his signature and to my amazement got it back—he wouldn't sign.—For a while I was bewildered by the blow, for it was an unpleasant surprise, very unpleasant!—The document was on the table in front of me and his letter was beside it. My eyes wandered in despair over the fatal lines which sealed my doom—it wasn't a death warrant, of course, because I could very easily have got others to sign, as many as I wanted really—but, as I've said, it was very, very unpleasant as it was; and as I sat there in my innocence I gradually fixed my glance on his signature, which in the right place could have made my future. It was an unusual hand—you know one can sit cluttering up a whole page with the most meaningless words. I had the pen in my hand—(*Takes the pen.*)—like this, and, somehow it started writing—I don't want to assert there was anything mystic—spiritualistic—back of it—I don't believe in that sort of thing!—It was a purely thoughtless mechanical process—when I sat copying that beautiful signature time and again—naturally without any intention of gaining anything by it. When I had covered the whole page, I had completely mastered writing his name—(*Throws away the pen.*)—and I forgot the whole thing. That night I slept heavily—and when I woke up, I had a feeling that I had been dreaming but couldn't remember the dream; sometimes it was as if a door had been opened slightly and I saw the desk with the promissory note as a reminder—and when I got up, I was driven to the desk absolutely as if after mature consideration I had made the irrevocable decision to write that name on the fatal document. All thoughts of consequences, of the risk had disappeared—there was no hesitation—it was almost as if I were carrying out a precious duty—and I wrote!—(*Jumps up.*) What can that have been? An impulse, a suggestion as it's called? But from whom? Why, I slept alone in my room! Could it have been my uncivilized self, the barbarian who doesn't recognize rules, who while my consciousness slept, stepped forward with his criminal will and his inability to calculate the consequences of an act? Tell me, what do you think?

MR. X (*worriedly*): Frankly, your story doesn't quite satisfy me—there are gaps, but that can be because you don't remember all the details now—and I have read one thing and another about criminal impulses. I seem to

remember—hm!—. But it doesn't matter—you've had
your punishment—and you had the courage to admit your
crime. We won't talk any more about it!

MR. Y: Yes, yes, yes, we're going to talk more about it, so that
I get full awareness of my innocence!

MR. X: Don't you have that?

MR. Y: No, I don't!

MR. X: Yes, you see that's what disturbs me! That's what
disturbs me!—Don't you think that every person has a
corpse in his cargo? Didn't we all steal and lie as children?
Yes, of course. Well, there are people who remain
children all their lives so that they can't control their
asocial desires. If the opportunity comes, the criminal's
ready!—But I can't understand why you don't feel you're
innocent! When the child is considered unaccountable, the
criminal should be, too.

It's strange—well, it doesn't matter, I'll probably regret
it later—(*Pause.*) I have killed a man, and I've never had
any pangs of conscience!

MR. Y (*extremely interested*): You————have?

MR. X: Yes, I have!—Maybe you want to take a murderer by
the hand?

MR. Y (*cheerfully*): Well, why not?

MR. X: But I haven't had my punishment!

MR. Y (*intimately, condescendingly*): All the better for
you!—How did you get out of it?

MR. X: There was no accuser, no suspicions, no witnesses. It
happened like this:—A friend had invited me one
Christmas to go hunting with him outside Uppsala. He
sent an old drunken sharecropper to meet me, the fellow
fell asleep on the driver's seat, got the rig caught in a
gateway, and turned it over in a ditch. I don't want to
blame being in danger of my life, but in an outburst of
impatience I finally gave him a kick in the throat to wake

him up, but with the result he never woke up but was dead on the spot!

MR. Y (*slyly*): Well-l, and you didn't report yourself?

MR. X: For these reasons: The man had no relatives or others for whom his life was important, he had lived out his time as a vegetable, his place could be taken right away by someone who needed it better; because of that and my being indispensable for my parents' happiness, for my own, and probably for science. Because of what happened I was cured of the desire to kick people, and just to satisfy abstract justice I had no wish to ruin my parents' and my lives!

MR. Y: So that's how you judge human worth?

MR. X: In that case, yes!

MR. Y: But the feeling of guilt, the balance, how about that?

MR. X: I didn't have any feeling of guilt, for I hadn't committed any crime. I had been kicked and had kicked as a boy, and it was only my ignorance about the effect of such acts on older people which caused his death.

MR. Y: Yes, but punishment for accidental murder is two years at hard labor—just the same as for—forging a signature.

MR. X: I've thought of that, too, you may believe! And many a night I've dreamt I was in prison! Ugh! Tell me, is it as hard as they say to be under lock and key?

MR. Y: Oh yes, it's hard.—First, they spoil your appearance by cutting off your hair so that if you didn't look like a criminal beforehand you would after that, and when you look in a mirror, you're convinced you're a bandit!

MR. X: It's your mask that's pulled off, probably! That's not badly calculated!

MR. Y: Go ahead, joke about it!—And they cut down on your food so that every day and hour you feel a definite difference between life and death! All the vital functions

are reduced, you feel how you're shrinking, and your soul
which was to be cured, rehabilitated, is put on a starvation
diet, is pressed back to the level of a thousand years ago;
you're allowed to read only things written for the
barbarians of the age of migrations, you get to hear only
about what will never happen in heaven; but what happens
on earth remains a secret; you're torn from your
environment, demoted from your class, put under the
control of inferiors, get illustrations of living in the bronze
age, feel as if you were wearing an animal skin, lived in a
cave, and ate out of a trough!

MR. X: Yes, but there's sense in that; for the one who behaves
as if he were from the bronze age should live in his
historical costume, I should think.

MR. Y (*furiously*): You're sneering! You who've acted like
someone from the stone age! But who gets to live in the
golden age anyway.

MR. X (*searchingly, sharply*): What do you mean—by the
golden age?

MR. Y (*slyly*): Nothing at all!

MR. X: You're lying—you're too cowardly to speak out fully!

MR. Y: Am I cowardly? You think so? I wasn't cowardly when
I dared to show up here where I've suffered as I
have.—But do you know what makes one suffer most
when one's locked up?—Well, it's this: that the others
aren't locked up, too!

MR. X: What others?

MR. Y: Those that haven't been punished!

MR. X: Are you referring to me?

MR. Y: Yes!

MR. X: I haven't committed a crime!

MR. Y: Is that so?

MR. X: No, an accident isn't a crime!

MR. Y: So murder's an accident?

MR. X: I haven't committed a murder!

MR. Y: So it isn't murder to kill someone?

MR. X: No, not always! There's manslaughter, unintentional homicide, assault leading to death, with subdivisions according to intent or lack of intent. But—now I'm really afraid for you—for you belong to the most dangerous category of human beings—the stupid ones!

MR. Y: So you're thinking I'm stupid! Listen! Do you want proof I'm very smart?

MR. X: Yes, tell me!

MR. Y: Will you admit I reason sensibly and logically when I say this: You had an accident that could have cost you two years at hard labor. You've been spared disgraceful punishment, completely. Here's a man—who has been the victim of a misfortune—an unconscious impulse—and has had to suffer through two years of punishment at hard labor. Only through great scientific achievements can this man wash away that spot which he involuntarily got on his reputation—but to attain those achievements he must have money—a lot of money—and money right away!

Don't you think the other man—the one who has not been punished—should restore the balance in human circumstances if he were sentenced to a reasonable penalty? Don't you think so?

MR. X (*calmly*): Yes!

MR. Y: Well, then we understand each other!—Hm! (*Pause.*) How much would you think is reasonable?

MR. X: Reasonable! The law puts the penalty at a minimum of fifty crowns. But since the dead man had no relatives, all talk about that matter is beside the point.

MR. Y: So, you don't want to understand! Then I'll speak more plainly: It's to me you're to pay the fine.

MR. X: I've never heard that killers should pay a penalty to forgers.—And there isn't any plaintiff here!

MR. Y: No?—Well—here you have me!

MR. X: Now it's getting clear!—How much do you want to become an accomplice in the murder?

MR. Y: Six thousand crowns!

MR. X: That's too much!—Where would I take them?
(MR. Y *points at the box.*)

MR. X: I don't want to do that! I don't want to become a thief!

MR. Y: Don't pretend! Do you want me to think you haven't dipped into that box before?

MR. X (*as if to himself*): To think I could be that wrong! But that's how it is with the soft ones! A person likes them, and believes so easily one is liked: and that's just why I've kept my eye on the ones I've liked!—So it's your conviction I've taken out of the box before?

MR. Y: Yes, of course!

MR. X: And now you're going to report me if you don't get six thousand crowns!

MR. Y: Absolutely! You can't get away from that, so you had better not try!

MR. X: You think I want to give my father a thief for a son, my wife a thief for a husband, my children a thief for a father, and my comrades a thief for a colleague! That's never going to happen!—Now I'll go to the sheriff to report myself!

MR. Y (*jumps up and gathers his things*): Wait a little!

MR. X: For what?

MR. Y (*stammering*): I only thought—that when I'm no longer needed—I wouldn't have to be present—and could be on my way!

MR. X: You may not!—Sit down where you sat by the table so we can talk a little first.

MR. Y (*sits down, after he has put on a dark coat*): Wh–, what's going to happen now?

MR. X (*looks in the mirror behind* MR. Y): Now I see!

MR. Y (*uneasily*): What do you see that's so special?

MR. X: I see in the mirror that you're a thief—a simple ordinary thief!—When you sat there before with your white shirt showing, I noticed only there was something wrong on my bookshelf, but I couldn't quite make out what, because I was listening to you, and observing you. Now since you became repulsive to me, I saw more clearly, and when you put on that black coat it contrasted with the red spine of the book, which didn't show up before because of your red suspenders, than I see you've been rereading the account of your forgery in Bernheim's dissertation about impulses and have put the book back upside down. So you stole the story, too!

Because of that, I think I have the right to conclude you committed your crime either out of need or for the pleasure of it!

MR. Y: Of need! If you knew—

MR. X: If *you* knew, in what need I've lived—and live! But that's not pertinent!—Further! That you've been in prison—that's almost certain; but it was in America, for it was prison life in America you told about; one thing more is almost certain: You didn't serve your sentence here.

MR. Y: How can you say that?

MR. X: Wait till the sheriff comes, you'll find out!

(MR. Y *gets up.*)

MR. X: You see! The first time I mentioned the sheriff in connection with the thunder, you wanted to take off! And when a person has been in prison, he never wants to go to a miller's hill every day to look at the prison or to stand back of a window pane—

In a word, you're both punished and unpunished! And that's why you were so exceptionally hard to get at! (*Pause.*)

MR. Y (*completely defeated*): May I go now?

MR. X: Now you may go!

MR. Y (*gathers his things*): Are you angry with me?

MR. X: Yes!—Do you like it better that I pity you?

MR. Y (*furiously*): Pity? Do you think you're better than I am?

MR. X: Of course I do since I am better than you! I have more sense than you and am more favorable toward property rights.

MR. Y: You're quite clever, but not as clever as I! I'm in check but the next move can checkmate you—all the same.

MR. X (*controls* MR. Y's *glance*): Shall we have another set to?—What evil do you intend to do?

MR. Y: That's my secret.

MR. X: May I look at you?—You're thinking of writing an anonymous letter to my wife to tell her my secret!

MR. Y: Yes, and you can't prevent that! You don't dare to have me locked up; so you have to let me go; and when I've gone, I can do what I want!

MR. X: You devil! You've hit my Achilles heel!—Do you want to force me to become a murderer?

MR. Y: You can't become that—you poor soul!

MR. X: You see, there's a difference between people! And you know that, you know I can't commit crimes like yours; so you have the upper hand. But think this over: what if you forced me to do to you what I did to the driver?(*Raises his hand as if to deliver such a blow.*)

MR. Y (*looks* MR. X *right in the eyes*): You can't! The one who can't save himself out of the box can't do that!

MR. X: So you don't think I've stolen out of the box?

MR. Y: You're too cowardly! Just as you were too cowardly to tell your wife that she's married to a murderer.

MR. X: You're a different kind of human being than I—stronger or weaker maybe—I don't know—more criminal or not—that doesn't concern me! but that you are more stupid, that's definite, for you were stupid when you forged a signature instead of begging—as I've had to do; you were stupid, when you stole out of my book—. Couldn't you grasp I had read my books?—You were stupid, when you believed you were more clever than I and that you could fool me into becoming a thief; you were stupid when you thought balance would be restored by giving the world two thieves instead of one and you were most stupid when you imagined I had gone about building my happiness without placing the cornerstone securely! Go ahead, write anonymous letters to my wife to tell her her husband is a murderer—she knew that before we got married! Do you give up?

MR. Y: May I go?

MR. X: Now you *are* going! Right now!—Your things behind you! Out!

[CURTAIN]

Simoon (Samum)

One Act

Characters

BISKRA, *an Arabian girl*
YOUSSEF, *her lover*
GUIMARD, *a Zouave lieutenant*

Setting

Algeria in our day {ca. 1890}

An Arabian marabout (sepulchre) with a sarcophagus in the middle of the floor. Prayer mats here and there; in the right corner a charnel house (an ossuary).

A door at the back with arches and drapes; round windows on the back wall. Small piles of sand here and there on the floor. An uprooted aloe, palm leaves, alfa grass in a pile.

BISKRA *enters with her burmoose hood pulled down over her face, a guitar on her back, throws herself down on a mat, and prays with her arms crossed over her chest. A wind is blowing outside.*

BISKRA: La ilâha ill allâh!

YOUSSEF (*enters hastily*): The Simoon's coming? Where's the Frenchman?

BISKRA: He'll be here in a minute!

YOUSSEF: Why didn't you kill him right away?

BISKRA: No! Because he's to do it himself! If I did it, the whites would kill our whole tribe—they know I was the guide Ali, though they don't know I'm the girl Biskra!

YOUSSEF: He's to do it himself? How?

BISKRA: You don't know the Simoon dries the white men's brains like dates and they get such terrifying hallucinations they find life so horrible they flee into the great unknown.

YOUSSEF: I've heard something like that—at the last encounter six Frenchmen took their lives before they got to their destination. But don't rely on Simoon today, for snow has fallen in the mountains and everything can be over in half an hour.—Biskra! Can you still hate?

139

BISKRA: Can I hate?—My hate is as boundless as the desert, scorching as the sun, and stronger than my love! Every hour of joy they've stolen from me since they killed Ali has gathered like poison under the rattlesnake's tooth, and what Simoon can't do, I can.

YOUSSEF: Well said, Biskra! And you'll do it. My hate has withered as grass in the fall since my eyes saw you. Take strength from me and be the arrow for my bow.

BISKRA: Take me in your arms, Youssef! Take me in your arms!

YOUSSEF: Not in this holy place! Now, now—later—when you've earned your reward!

BISKRA: Proud sheik, proud man!

YOUSSEF: Yes, the girl who's to carry my offspring under her heart must be worthy of that honor!

BISKRA: I—no one else—will carry your offspring! I, Biskra—despised, ugly, but strong!

YOUSSEF: Well then! Now I'm going down by the spring to sleep!—Do I need to teach you the secret arts which the great Marabout [Saint] Siddi-sheik taught you, and which you have practiced at market fairs ever since you were a child?

BISKRA: No, you don't—I know all the secrets needed to frighten the life out of a cowardly Frenchman, the coward who steals up on his enemy and sends the bullet ahead of him! I know all of them—even ventriloquism. And what my tricks won't do, the sun will—the sun's on our side.

YOUSSEF: The sun is the Muslim's friend, but can't be relied on. You can burn yourself, girl! Have a drink of water first, for I see your hands are wrinkled and—(*He has lifted a mat, opened a trapdoor, and goes down for a bowl of water which he hands* BISKRA.)

BISKRA (*lifts the bowl to her mouth*): —And my eye's beginning to see red—my lungs are drying up—I hear—I hear—do

you see the sand already running through the ceiling—
and the strings of the guitar are humming—Simoon is
here! But the Frenchman isn't!

YOUSSEF: Come down here, Biskra, and let the Frenchman
die by himself!

BISKRA: First Hell and then Death! Do you think I'd fail?
(*Pours the water on a pile of sand.*) I'll water the sand so
vengeance will grow! And I'll let my heart dry up! Grow,
hate! Burn, sun! Choke, wind!

YOUSSEF: Hail, Ibn Youssef's mother, for you're going to
bear my son, the avenger! You!

(*The wind increases; the drape in front of the door moves; a
red glow lights up the room but turns to yellow in the following
scene.*)

BISKRA: The Frenchman's coming, and—Simoon's
here!—Go!

YOUSSEF: I'll see you in half an hour! There's the sun dial!
(*Points at a sand pile.*) Heaven itself metes out time for the
unbelievers' hell!

(GUIMARD *enters, pale and staggering, confused, talks
almost in a whisper.*)

GUIMARD: Simoon's here!—where do you think my people
have gone?

BISKRA: I led your people west to east!

GUIMARD: West to—east!—Let me see!—That's straight
east—and west!—Give me a chair and a glass of water!

BISKRA (*leads* GUIMARD *to the sand pile, has him lie down with
his head on the sandpile*): Are you sitting comfortably so?

GUIMARD (*looks at her*): I'm sitting a little crooked. Put
something under my head.

BISKRA (*stacks up the sand under his head*): There, you have a
pillow under your head!

GUIMARD: My head? Why, that's my feet!—Aren't my feet
there?

BISKRA: Of course!

GUIMARD: I thought so!—Give me a stool under—my head!

BISKRA (*drags the aloe over and puts it under* GUIMARD's *knees*):
There's a stool for you!

GUIMARD: And water!—Water!

BISKRA (*takes the empty bowl, fills it with sand, and hands it to*
GUIMARD): Drink this while it's cold!

GUIMARD (*sips at the bowl*): It *is* cold—but it still doesn't
quench my thirst!—I can't drink—I detest water—take it
away!

BISKRA: There's the dog that bit you!

GUIMARD: What dog? I've never been bitten by any dog.

BISKRA: Simoon has shrunk your memory—watch out for
Simoon's illusion! You remember the mad greyhound
that bit you the next to last hunt in Bab-el-Ouëd.

GUIMARD: The hunt at Bab-el-Ouëd! That's right! Was it
brown like a beaver?

BISKRA: A bitch? Yes! You see! And he bit you in the calf!
Can't you feel the sore hurt?

GUIMARD (*touches his calf, scratches himself on the aloe*): Yes, I
can feel the pain!—Water! Water!

BISKRA (*handing him the bowl of sand*): Drink! Drink!

GUIMARD: No, I can't! Mary, Mother of God,—I've got the
horrors!

BISKRA: Don't be afraid! I'll heal you and drive out the
demon with the omnipotence of music! Listen!

GUIMARD (*screams*): Ali! Ali! Not music! I can't stand it! And
what use would it be for me?

BISKRA: If Music tames the wily spirit of the serpent, don't
you think it can manage a mad dog? Listen! (*Sings
accompanying herself on the guitar.*)
Biskra—Biskra, Biskra—Biskra, Biskra—Biskra.
Simoon!   Simoon!

YOUSSEF (*from below*): Simoon! Simoon!

GUIMARD: What's that you're singing? Ali!

BISKRA: Have I been singing? See, now I'm taking a palmleaf in my mouth! (*Takes a palmbranch between her teeth.*)

SONG (*from above*): Biskra-Biskra, Biskra-Biskra, Biskra, Biskra.

YOUSSEF (*from below*): Simoon! Simoon!

GUIMARD: What a hellish illusion!

BISKRA *and* YOUSSEF (*together*): Biskra-Biskra, Biskra-Biskra, Biskra-Biskra, Simoon!

GUIMARD (*struggles to his feet*): Who are you, you devil singing with two voices? Are you a man or a woman? Or both?

BISKRA: I am Ali, the guide! You don't recognize me, because your senses are confused; but if you want to save yourself from the illusions of sight and thought believe me, believe what I say and do as I say.

GUIMARD: You don't need to ask me to, for I find everything *is* as you say it is!

BISKRA: You see that, you idol worshipper!

GUIMARD: Idol worshipper?

BISKRA: Yes, take out that idol you're wearing on your chest! (*He takes out a medal.*) Trample it underfoot, and call on the only God, the merciful, the compassionate!

GUIMARD (*hesitating*): It's St. Edward, my patron saint!

BISKRA: Can he protect you? Can he?

GUIMARD: No, he can't!—(*Comes to.*) Yes, he can!

BISKRA: Let me see that! (*She opens the door, the curtain flutters, and the grass waves.*)

GUIMARD (*covering his mouth*): Shut the door!

BISKRA: Down with the idol!

GUIMARD: No, I can't!

BISKRA: See! Simoon doesn't bend one hair on me, but you, the infidel, he kills! Down with the idol!

GUIMARD (*throws the medal on the floor*): Water! I'm dying!

BISKRA: Pray to the only God, the merciful, the compassionate!

GUIMARD: How shall I pray?

BISKRA: Say what I say!

GUIMARD: Speak!

BISKRA: God is one, there is no other God but He, the merciful, the compassionate!

GUIMARD: "God is one, there is no other God but He, the merciful, the compassionate!"

BISKRA: Lie down on the floor! (*He lies down on the floor unwillingly.*) What do you hear?

GUIMARD: A spring gurgling!

BISKRA: See! God is one, and there is no other than He, the merciful, the compassionate!—What do you see?

GUIMARD: I see a spring gurgling—I hear a lamp shining—in a window with green shutters—by a white street—

BISKRA: Who's sitting by the window?

GUIMARD: My wife—Elise!

BISKRA: Who's standing back of the curtain putting his arm about her?

GUIMARD: It's my son—Georges!

BISKRA: How old is your son?

GUIMARD: Four years next St. Nicholas Day!

BISKRA: And he can already stand back of a curtain holding his arm about another man's wife?

GUIMARD: No, he can't—but it *is* he!

BISKRA: Four years old with a blond moustache!

GUIMARD: A blond moustache, you say!—Ah, it is—my friend, Jules!

BISKRA: Who's standing back of the curtain with his arm about your wife!

GUIMARD: That devil!

BISKRA: Do you see your son?

GUIMARD: No, not any more!

BISKRA (*imitates the tolling of bells on her guitar*): What do you see now?

GUIMARD: I see bells tolling—I feel the taste of dead bodies—my mouth smells like rancid butter—ugh!

BISKRA: Don't you hear the curate singing at a child's funeral?

GUIMARD: Wait!—I can't hear that—(*Sadly*) but do you want me to?—then—now I hear it!

BISKRA: Do you see the wreath on the coffin they're carrying out?

GUIMARD: Yes—

BISKRA: It has purple bands—and it says in silver letters—"Farewell, my beloved Georges—your father."

GUIMARD: Yes, that's what it says! (*Weeps.*) My Georges! Georges! My dear child!—Elise, my wife, comfort me!—Help me! (*Fumbles about.*) Where are you? Elise! Have you left me? Answer me! Call out the name of the man you love!

VOICE (*from the ceiling*): Jules, Jules!

GUIMARD: Jules!—Why, my name's—What is my name?—It is Charles!—And she called Jules!—Elise—beloved wife—answer me, for your spirit is here—I feel it—and you promised you would never love anyone else—

(VOICE *laughs.*)

GUIMARD: Who's laughing?

BISKRA: Elise! Your wife!

GUIMARD: Kill me!—I don't want to live any longer! Life nauseates me as sour cabbage in lard—do you know what lard is? Swine fat! (*Spits.*) I haven't any saliva anymore—water! Water! Or I'll bite you! (*Full storm outside.*)

BISKRA (*covers her mouth and coughs*): Now you're dying, Frenchman! Draw up your last will while there's time!—Where's your notebook?

GUIMARD (*takes out his notebook and a pen*): What shall I write?

BISKRA: A man thinks of his wife when he's dying—and of his children!

GUIMARD (*writes*): "Elise—I curse you! Simoon—I'm dying—"

BISKRA: And sign it or it won't be legal!

GUIMARD: What?

BISKRA: Write: La ilàha ill allàh!

GUIMARD: It is written! May I die now?

BISKRA: Now you may die, like a cowardly soldier, who has deserted his people!—And you'll probably get a nice funeral with the jackals, who will sing when they carry you out!

Do you hear the drum—signaling attack—the infidels who have the sun and Simoon on their side advance—out of ambushes—(*Strums the guitar.*)—the shots are fired along the whole line—the Frenchmen can't reload—the Arabians shoot in scattered array—the Frenchmen flee!

GUIMARD (*rises*): Frenchmen do not flee!

BISKRA (*sounds "retreat" on a flute she has taken up*): The Frenchmen flee when it sounds retreat!

GUIMARD: They're drawing back—that's the retreat—and I am here—(*Tears off his epaulets*) I am dead! (*Falls down on the floor.*)

BISKRA: Yes, you are dead!—You don't know that you have been for a long time! (*Goes to the charnel house, picks up a skull.*)

GUIMARD: Have I been dead? (*Touches his face.*)

BISKRA: For a long, long time!—Look at yourself in the mirror! (*Shows him the skull.*)

GUIMARD: Ah! That's I!

BISKRA: Don't you see your protruding cheeks—don't you see how the vultures have eaten your eyes—don't you recognize the hole from your right molar you had pulled—don't you see the little hollow in your chin where the little pointed beard grew that your Elise liked to play with—don't you see where the ear was, the ear Georges used to kiss mornings at the coffee table—don't you see where the axe hit—when the hangman executed the deserter?——

(GUIMARD *who has watched and listened to her in horror falls down dead.*)

BISKRA (*who has been kneeling, gets up, after she has felt his pulse. Sings*): Simoon! Simoon! (*Opens the doors, the drapes flutter, she covers her mouth and falls backwards*) Youssef! (*Youssef comes up from the cellar, examines* GUIMARD, *and looks for* BISKRA.)

YOUSSEF: Biskra! (*Sees her, lifts her in his arms*) Are you alive?

BISKRA: Is the Frenchman dead?

YOUSSEF: If he isn't, he will be! Simoon! Simoon!

BISKRA: Then I'm alive! But give me water!

YOUSSEF (*carries her toward the trapdoor*): Here!—Now Youssef is yours!

BISKRA: And Biskra will be your son's mother! Youssef, Youssef!

YOUSSEF: You're strong, Biskra! Stronger than Simoon!

[CURTAIN]